The
Re-Conquest
of Ireland

James Connolly

This book has been published by:

Contact: sales@nuvisionpublications.com

URL: http://www.nuvisionpublications.com

Publishing Date: 2007

ISBN# 1-59547-899-X

Please see my website for several books created for
education, research and entertainment.

Specializing in rare, out-of-print books still in demand.

Table of Contents

Foreword

"The conquest of Ireland had meant the social and political servitude of the Irish masses, and therefore the re-conquest of Ireland must mean the social as well as the political independence from servitude of every man, woman and child in Ireland."

The underlying idea of this work is that the Labour Movement of Ireland must set itself the Re-Conquest of Ireland as its final aim, that that re-conquest involves taking possession of the entire country, all its power of wealth-production and all its natural resources, and organising these on a co-operative basis for the good of all. To demonstrate that this and this alone would be a re-conquest, the attempt is made to explain what the Conquest of Ireland was, how it affected the Catholic natives and the Protestant settlers, how the former were subjected and despoiled by open force, and how the latter were despoiled by fraud, and when they protested were also subjected by force, and how out of this common spoliation and subjection there arises to-day the necessity of common action to reverse the Conquest, in order that the present population, descendants alike of the plebeian Conquerors and the Conquered plebeians, may enjoy in common fraternity and good-will that economic security and liberty for which their ancestors fought, or thought they fought.

The United Irishmen at the end of the Eighteenth Century in an address to the conflicting religious sects of Ireland declared:–

We wish that our animosities were buried with the bones of our ancestors, and that we could *unite* as Citizens and claim the Rights of Man.

We echo that wish to-day, and add that the first social right of man is to live, and that he cannot enjoy that right whilst the means of life for all are the private property of a class. This little book, as a picture of the past and present social conditions of the Irish masses, seeks to drive that lesson home, and to present to the reader some of the results which have followed in Ireland the capitalistic denial of that human social right.

7

Chapter I

The Conquest of Ireland

Before we can talk of or develop a policy for the re-conquest of Ireland it is well that we picture clearly to our mind the essential feature of the conquest itself, how far it went, and how far it has already been reversed. Let it be remembered, then, that the conquest was two-fold – social and political. It was the imposition upon Ireland of an alien rule in political matters and of a social system equally alien and even more abhorrent.

In the picturesque phrase of Fintan Lalor it meant the "conquest of our liberties and the conquest of our lands". The lands being the material basis of life, alike of conquerors and conquered, whosoever held those lands was master of the lives and liberties of the nation. The full extent of that mastery, that conquest, is best seen by the record of the Cromwellian settlement in 1654. In that settlement the conquest reached its highest and completest point. Never before, and never again, were the lives and liberties of the people of Ireland so completely at the mercy of foreign masters as during the period in question.

Previously the old Gaelic culture and social system still held sway in the greater part of Ireland, and the armed force of the Gael still existed to curb the greed of the alien enemy and restrain, by the example of its greater freedom, the full exercise of his tyrannical propensities, and subsequently the gradual growth of the ideals of a softer civilisation, and the growth of democracy, contributed to weaken the iron rule of the conqueror. But the Cromwellian settlement well understood was indeed the final consummation of the conquest of Ireland. There are then three pictures we must needs conjure up before our mind's eye in our endeavour to understand the point we have reached in the history of the Irish nation. These three pictures are successively – of Ireland as she was before the conquest; as she was at the completion of the conquest; as she will be at the re-conquest by the people of Ireland of their own country. The first is a picture of a country in which the people of the island were owners of the land upon which they lived, masters of their

9

own lives and liberties, freely electing their rulers, and shaping their castes and conventions to permit of the closest approximation to their ideals of justice as between man and man. It is a picture of a system of society in which all were knit together as in a family, in which all were members having their definite place, and in which the highest could not infringe upon the rights of the lowest – those rights being as firmly fixed and assured as the powers of the highest, and fixed and assured by the same legal code and social convention. It is a system evolved through centuries of development out of the genius of the Irish race, safeguarded by the swords of Irishmen, and treasured in the domestic affections of Irish women.

The second picture is a picture of the destruction by force of the native system and the dispersion and enslavement of the natives. Let these few quotations from Prendergast's *Cromwellian Settlement of Ireland* place before our eyes this picture in all its grim and agonising horror. He tells of the proclamation issued by the English Parliament directing that "by beat of drum and sound of trumpet, on some market day within ten days after the same shall come unto them within their respective precincts", the English governors throughout Ireland shall proclaim that "all the ancient estates and farms of the people of Ireland were to belong to the adventurers and the army of England, and that the Parliament had assigned Connaught for the habitation of the Irish nation, whither they must transplant their wives and daughters and children before the First of May following (1654) under penalty of death if found on this side of the Shannon after that day".

In addition to this transplanting to Connacht, gangs of soldiery were despatched throughout Ireland to kidnap young boys and girls of tender years to be sold into slavery in the West Indies. Sir William Petty, ancestor of the Lansdowne family and a greedy and unscrupulous land-thief, declared that in some Irish accounts the number so sold into slavery was estimated at one hundred thousand.

This ancestor of Lord Lansdowne, the founder of the noble Lansdowne family, Sir William Petty, landed in Ireland in 1652 with a total capital of all his fortune of £500. But he came over in the wake of Cromwell's army, and got himself appointed 'Physician to the Army of Ireland'. In 1662 he was made one of a Court of Commissioners of Irish Estates, and also Surveyor-General for Ireland. As the native Irish were then being hunted to death, or transported in slave-gangs to Barbadoes, the latter fact gave this worthy ancestor of a worthy lord excellent opportunities to 'invest' his £500 to good purpose.

How this hunting of the Irish was going on whilst Sir William Petty was founding the noble Lansdowne family may be gauged from the fact that over 100,000 men, women and children were transported to the West Indies, there to be sold into slavery upon the tobacco plantations. Prendergast, in his *Cromwellian Settlement of Ireland*, gives the following illustration of the methods pursued:–

10

"As an instance out of many:– Captain John Vernon was employed by the Commissioners for Ireland to England, and contracted in their behalf with Mr. David Sellick and the Leader under his hand to supply them with two hundred and fifty women of the Irish nation, above twelve years and under the age of forty-five, also three hundred men above twelve years and under fifty, to be found in the country within twenty miles of Cork, Youghal and Kinsale, Waterford and Wexford, to transport them into New England."

This Bristol firm alone was responsible for shipping over 6,400 girls and boys, one of their agents in the County Cork being Lord Broghill, afterwards Earl of Orrery.

Every Irishman or woman not able to hide in the woods, morasses or mountains, or not able to defend themselves by force of arms, was good prey at that time, and hence, when Sir William Petty coveted a piece of land, he but required to send a party of *soldiers* to hunt down the owners or occupants, ship them out to the West Indies as slaves, and lo! the trick was done. The land was thenceforth the property of the Lord's anointed. So when Sir William Petty died the original £500 with which he came to Ireland had swelled to an annual rent roll of £18,000, and from one mountain peak in the County Kerry he could look round and see no land that had not fallen into his grasp.

Here then is the conquest. Fix it clearly before your eyes. National liberty, personal liberty, social security all gone; the country ruled from its highest down to its meanest officer by foreigners; the Irish race landless, homeless, living by sufferance upon the mercy of their masters, or trusting alone to the greed of their conquerors to gain that toleration which even a conqueror must give to the slaves whose labour he requires to sate his avarice or minister to his wants.

This, then, is the second picture. Mastery of the lives and liberties of the people of Ireland by forces outside of and irresponsible and unresponsive to the people of Ireland – social and political slavery.

The third picture must be drawn by each, as it suits his or her fancy, who wishes to visualise to the mind's eye the complete reversal of all that was embodied in the second. As they construct that picture of the future so they will shape their public actions. In the belief that the labour movement alone has an ideal involving the complete reversal of the social and political consequences defined in the second picture, these chapters were written to help the workers in constructing that mental picture aright.

But how far has that conquest been already reversed? As a cold historical fact that conquest fell far short of the impious wishes of its projectors. The projected removal of the entire people to within the confines of Connacht came into collision with the desires of the land-thieves for a tenantry upon whose labours they could grow rich. Land without labour is valueless; and to be an owner of confiscated land, and that land lying idle for want of labourers did not suit the desires of the new Cromwellian squire-archy. So gradually the laws were relaxed or their evasion connived at by the local rulers, and the peasantry began to re-appear at or near their former homes, and eventually to gain permission to be tenants and labourers to the new masters. Into the towns the Catholic also began to find his way as a personal servant, or in some other menial way ministering to the needs of his new rulers.

Catholic women were within the forbidden territory as wives of Protestant officers or soldiers, and by rearing up their children in their own faith, whispering old legends into their ears by day, or crooning old Gaelic songs to them at night helped, consciously or unconsciously, to re-create an Irish atmosphere in the very heart of the ascendancy. Ere long, by one of those silent movements of which the superficial historian takes no account, the proscribed people were once more back from the province into which they had been hunted, heartbroken and subdued, it is true, but nevertheless back upon their own lands.

In the North the proscription had been more effectual for the reason that in that province there were Protestant settlers to occupy the lands from which the Catholics had been driven. But even there the craving for a return to the old homes and tribelands destroyed the full effect of the Cromwellian proscription. The hunted Ulstermen and women crept back from Connacht and, unable to act like their Southern brethren and re-occupy their own lands upon any terms, they took refuge in the hills and 'mountainy' land. At first we can imagine these poor people led a somewhat precarious life, ever dreading the advent of a Government force to dislodge them and drive them back to Connacht; but they persisted, built their huts, tilled with infinite toil the poor soil from which they scraped the accumulations of stones, and gradually established their families in the position of a tolerated evil. Two things helped in securing this toleration.

First, the avarice of the new land-owning aristocracy, who easily subdued their religious fanaticism sufficiently to permit Papists settling upon and paying rent for formerly worthless mountain land.

Second, the growing acuteness of the difficulties of the Government in England itself; the death of Cromwell; the fear of the owners of confiscated estates that the accession of Charles II might lead to a resumption of their property by former owners, and, arising from that fear, a disinclination to attract too much attention by further attacks upon the returning Catholics, who might retaliate, and, finally, the unrest and general uncertainty centering round the succession to the throne.

Thus, in Ulster the Celt returned to his ancient tribelands, but to its hills and stony fastnesses, from which with tear-dimmed eyes he could look down upon the fertile plains of his fathers which he might never again hope to occupy, even on sufferance.

On the other hand, the Protestant common soldier or settler, now that the need of his sword was passed, found himself upon the lands of the Catholic, it is true, but solely as a tenant and dependant. The ownership of the province was not in his hands, but in the hands of the companies of London merchants who had supplied the sinews of war for the English armies, or, in the hands of the greedy aristocrats and legal cormorants who had schemed and intrigued while he had fought. The end of the Cromwellian settlement then found the 'commonality', to use a good old word, dispossessed and defrauded of all hold upon the soil of Ireland – the Catholic dispossessed by force, the Protestant dispossessed by fraud. Each hating and blaming the other, a situation which the dominant aristocracy knew well how, as their descendants know to-day, to profit by to their own advantage.

This, then was the Conquest. Now sit down and calmly reason out to yourself how far we have gone to the reversal of that conquest – how far we have still to go. The measure of our progress towards its reversal is the measure of the progress of democracy in this island, as measured by the upward march of the 'lower classes'. The insurgence of the peasantry against the landlord, the shattering of the power of the landlord, the surrender of the British Government to the demand for the abolition of landlordism, all were so many steps toward the replanting securely upon the soil of Ireland of that population which, "with sound of trumpett and beat of drumme", were ordered 300 years ago "with their women and daughters and children" to betake themselves across the Shannon into Connacht, there to remain for ever as the despised and hated helots of foreign masters.

The unsatisfactory nature of the scheme for replanting may be admitted; the essential fact is the reversal of that part of the conquest which demanded and enforced the uprooting and expropriation and dispersion of the mere Irish. In this, as in the political and social world generally, the thing that matters most is not so much the *extent* of our march, but rather the *direction* in which we are marching.

On the political side the Re-conquest of Ireland by its people has gone on even more exhaustively and rapidly. We remember sitting as delegates to the ''98 Centenary Committee' in the Council Room of the City Hall of Dublin in 1898, and looking around upon the pictures of the loyal ascendancy Lord Mayors of the past which cover the walls of that room. At first we thought merely that if the dead do have cognisance of the acts of the living, surely fierce and awful must be the feelings of these old tyrants at the thought that such a room should be handed over gratuitously to the use of such rebels as were there upon that occasion. Then our thoughts took a wider range, and we went in imagination back to that period we have spoken of as the culmination of the Conquest, and forward to the following year when we were assured that under the Local Government Act the representatives of the labourers of Ireland might sit and legislate all over Ireland in such halls of local power as the Council Room of the Municipality of Dublin. What a revolution was here! At the one period banished, proscribed, and a serf even to the serfs of his masters; at the other period quietly invading all the governing boards of the land, pushing out the old aristocracy and installing in their places the sons of toil fresh from field, farm and workshop, having the legal right to grasp every position of political power, local administration and responsibility – where at the former period they were hunted animals whose lives were not accounted as valuable as foxes or hares. Truly this was, and is, a rolling back of the waves of conquest. But how many had or have the imagination necessary to grasp the grandeur of this slow re-instatement of a nation, and how many or how few can realise that we are now witnessing another such change, chiefly portentous to us as a still further development of the grasp of the Irish democracy upon the things that matter in the life of a people.

It shall be our task in future chapters briefly to portray that development, to picture how far we have gone, to illustrate the truth that the capitalist and landlord classes in Ireland, irrespective of their political creed, are still saturated with the spirit of the conquest, and that it is only in the working class we may expect to find the true principles of action, which, developed into a theory, would furnish a real philosophy of Irish freedom.

But in this, as in many other conflicts, the philosophy of Irish freedom will probably, for the great multitude, follow the lines of battle rather than precede them. The thinking few may, and should, understand the line of march; the many will fight from day to day, and battle to battle, as their class instincts and immediate needs compel them.

For the writer, our inspiration, we confess, comes largely from the mental contemplation of these two pictures. The dispossessed Irish race dragging itself painfully along through roads, mountains and morasses, footsore and bleeding, at the behest of a merciless conqueror, and the same race in the near future marching confidently and serenely, aided by all the political and social machinery they can wrest from the hands of their masters, to the re-conquest of Ireland.

Chapter II

Ulster and the Conquest

In the foregoing chapter we have dwelt with the consequence of the Conquest of Ireland as it affected the Celtic or Catholic Irish and endeavoured to demonstrate to readers that the duty that now lies upon the Irish working-class democracy is in the nature of a reversal of that Conquest and all that it implies. That, in short, every step taken towards making the wealth-producing powers of the country the common property of the Irish people, though it may be decried in the name of patriotism by the spokesmen of the privileged classes, is yet in effect a step towards the reversal of the Conquest and the re-establishment of the ancient freedom upon a modern basis. But it remains to be discussed how and in what manner the Conquest affected the rank and file of the armies of the conquerors, how they and their descendants fared as a result of their adventures. This is all the more important because the children of these men of the rank and file are now an integral part of the Irish nation, and their interests and well-being are now as vital to the cause of freedom and as sacred in the eyes of the Labour Movement as are the interests of the descendants of those upon whom a cruel destiny compelled their forefathers to make war. If in this brief setting forth of the position of the working-class democracy in Ireland we have to refer to the question of religion, it is not in order that divisions upon these lines may be perpetuated, but rather that it may be learned that, despite diversity of origin, the historical development of Ireland has brought the same social slavery to the whole of the workers, let their religion have been or be what it may. Certainly the opinion implied in the existence of sectarian political societies in Ireland is that religious ideas, or rather varying beliefs upon religion, were the real basis of past Irish politics, and the Orangemen are told that the Orange festivals of to-day are commemorations of great victories won by their leaders in the cause of 'civil and religious liberty'.

The belief we acquire from a more dispassionate study of history in Ireland is somewhat different. Let us tell it briefly:–

In the reign of James I the English Government essayed to solve the Irish problem, which then, as now, was their chief trouble, by settling Ireland with planters from Scotland and England. To do this, two million acres were confiscated – stolen from the Irish owners. Froude, the historian, says:–

Of these, a million and a half, bog-forest and mountain were restored to the Irish. The half a million of fertile acres were settled with families of Scottish and English Protestants.

A friendly speaker, recently describing these planters before a meeting of the Belfast Liberal Association, spoke of them as:–

Hardy pioneers, born of a sturdy race, trained to adversity, when brought face to face with dangers of a new life in a hostile country, soon developed that steady, energetic, and powerful character which has made the name of Ulster respected all over the world.

But Mr. W.T. Lattimer, the author of a *History of Irish Presbyterianism*, speaking of the same planters states on page 43 of his book:–

Amongst these settlers were so many who left their country for their country's good, that it was common to say regarding anyone not doing well that his latter end would be "Ireland".

And a writer in the seventeenth century, the son of one of the ministers who came over with the first plantation, Mr. Stewart, is quoted by Lecky in his *History of England in the Eighteenth Century*, as saying:–

From Scotland came many, and from England not a few, yet all of them generally the scum of both nations, who from debt or breaking of the law, came hither hoping to be without fear of man's justice in a land where there was nothing, or but little as yet, of the fear of God. On all hands Atheism increased and disregard of God, iniquity abounded with contentious fighting, murder, adultery.

The reader can take his choice of these descriptions. Probably the truth is that each is a fairly accurate description of a section of the planters, and that neither is accurate as a picture of the whole.

But while the Plantation succeeded from the point of view of the Government in placing in the heart of Ulster a body of people who, whatever their disaffection to that Government, were still bound by fears of their own safety to defend it against the natives, it did not bring either civil or religious liberty to the Presbyterian planters.

The Episcopalians were in power, and all the forces of government were used by them against their fellow-Protestants. The planters were continually harassed to make them abjure their religion, fines were multiplied upon fines, and imprisonment upon imprisonment. In 1640 the Presbyterians of Antrim, Down, and Tyrone in a petition to the English House of Commons declared that:–

Principally through the sway of the prelacy with their factions, our souls are starved, our estates are undone, our families impoverished, and many lives among us cut off and destroyed. Our cruel taskmasters have made us, who were once a people, to become as it were no people, an astonishment to ourselves, the object of pittie and amazement to others.

What might have been the result of this cruel systematic persecution of Protestants by Protestants we can only conjecture, since, in the following year, 1641, the great Irish rebellion compelled the persecuting and persecuted Protestants to join hands in defence of their common plunder against the common enemy – the original Irish owners.

In all the demonstrations and meetings which take place in Ulster under Orange auspices, all these persecutions are alluded to as if they had been the work of 'Papists', and even in the Presbyterian churches and conventions the same distortion of the truth is continually practised. But, they are told "all this persecution was ended when William of Orange, and our immortal forefathers overthrew the Pope and Popery at the Boyne. Then began the era of civil and religious liberty".

So runs the legend implicitly believed in in Ulster. Yet it is far, very far, from the truth. In 1686 certain continental powers joined together in a league, known in history as the league of Augsburg, for the purpose of curbing the arrogant power of France. These powers were impartially Protestant and Catholic, including the Emperor of Germany, the King of Spain, William Prince of Orange, and the Pope. The latter had but a small army, but possessed a good treasury and great influence. A few years before, a French army had marched upon Rome to avenge a slight insult offered to France, and His Holiness was more than anxious to curb the Catholic power that had dared to violate the centre of Catholicity. Hence his alliance with William Prince of Orange. In his *History of Civilisation* Guizot, the French Protestant Historian, says of this League:–

The League was so powerful against Louis XIV that openly or in a hidden but very real manner, sovereigns were seen to enter it who were assuredly very far from being interested in favour of civil or religious liberty. The Emperor of Germany and Pope Innocent XI supported William III against Louis XIV.

King James II of England, being insecure upon his throne, sought alliance with the French Monarch.

When, therefore, the war took place in Ireland, King William fought, aided by the arms, men, and treasuries of his allies in the league of Augsburg, and part of his expenses at the Battle of the Boyne was paid for by His Holiness, the Pope. Moreover, when news of King William's victory reached Rome a *Te Deum* was sung in celebration of his victory over the Irish adherents of King James and King Louis. Similar celebrations were also held at the great Catholic capitals of Madrid and Brussels.

Nor did victory at the Boyne mean Civil and Religious Liberty! The Catholic Parliament of King James, meeting in Dublin in 1689, had passed a law that all religions were equal, and that each clergyman should be supported by his own congregation only, and that no tithes should be levied upon any man for the support of a church to which he did not belong. But this sublime conception was far from being entertained by the Williamites who overthrew King James and superseded his Parliament. The Episcopalian Church was immediately re-established, and all other religions put under the ban of the law. I need not refer to the Penal Laws against Catholics, they are well enough known. It it sufficient to point out that England and Wales have not yet attained to that degree of religious equality established by Acts XIII and XV of the Catholic Parliament of 1689, and that that date was the last in which Catholics and Protestants sat together in Parliament until the former compelled an Emancipation Act in 1829.

Mr. Fisher in an introductory note to his book, *The End of the Irish Parliament*, thus describes the position of the Irish people, Protestant and Catholic, after the overthrow of the Irish forces and the breach of the Articles in the Treaty of Limerick granting religious toleration:–

Not only were the representatives of Roman Catholics expressly excluded, but even the members of the Scottish colony in the North were, for the greater part of the eighteenth century, proscribed and excluded from equal civil rights by an obnoxious test which no loyal member of the Scottish Church could take.

As Mr. Fisher is a modern author of unimpeachable loyalty and opposition to all things savouring of Catholicity, Nationalism and Socialism, his evidence is valuable for the sake of those unable or unwilling to undertake the work of personal investigation of older authorities.

For the Presbyterians, the victory at the Boyne simply gave a freer hand to their Episcopalian persecutors. In 1691, after the accession of William III, a Presbterian minister was liable to three months in the common jail for delivering a sermon, and to a fine of £100 for celebrating the Lord's Supper.

In 1704 Derry was rewarded for its heroic defence by being compelled to submit to a Test Act, which shut out of all offices in the Law, the

Army, the Navy, the Customs and Excise and Municipal employment, all who would not conform to the Episcopalian Church. Ten aldermen and fourteen burgesses are said to have been disfranchised in the Maiden City by this iniquitous Act, which was also enforced all over Ireland. Thus, at one stroke, Presbyterians, Quakers and all other dissenters were deprived of what they had imagined they were fighting for.

After Derry, Aughrim and the Boyne, Presbyterians, Unitarians, Quakers, and all other dissenters from the Episcopalian Church were thus shut out from representation in any parliamentary borough. They were excluded from all seats in the Corporation, even in such places as Belfast where they then formed almost the entire population; in fact it is even alleged by Protestant writers that at that time greater toleration was shown by King William's government and its immediate successor to Catholics than to Protestant dissenters from Episcopacy.

Presbyterians were forbidden to be married by their own clergymen, the Ecclesiastical Courts had power to fine and imprison offenders, and to compel them to appear in the Parish Church, and make public confession of fornication, if so married. At Lisburn and Tullyish, Presbyterians were actually punished for being married by their own ministers. Some years later, in 1772, a number of Presbyterians were arrested for attempting to establish a Presbyterian meeting house in Belturbet.

In 1713 the Presbyterians attempted to secure a foot-hold in Drogheda. Their rivals, the Episcopalians, took alarm and, upon a Presbyterian missionary, the Rev. James Fleming, of Lurgan, proceeding to Drogheda, he and three of his co-religionists in that town were arrested and committed to stand trial at the Assizes for 'riot and unlawful assembly', said offence having taken the form of a prayer meeting on Presbyterian lines. The Rev. William Biggar was also, in the following week, committed to prison for three months for the same 'offense'. Rev. Alexander McCracken of Lisburn was fined £500 and committed to six months' imprisonment as a 'non-juror'.

In the same year an Act passed in the English Parliament made Presbyterian schoolmasters liable to three months' imprisonment for teaching. The marriage of a Presbyterian and an Episcopalian was declared illegal; in fact the ministers and congregations of the former church were treated as outlaws and rebels, to be fined, imprisoned, and harassed in every possible way. They had to pay tithes for the upkeep of the Episcopalian ministers, were fined for not going to the Episcopalian Church, and had to pay Church cess for buying Sacramental bread, ringing the bell, and washing the surplices of the Episcopalian clergymen. All this, remember, in the generation immediately following the Battle of the Boyne.

19

Upon this point the testimony of the great anti-Catholic historian and champion of the propertied classes, Froude, is very interesting. He says:-

Vexed with suits in the ecclesiastical courts, forbidden to educate their children in their own faith, treated as dangerous to a State which but for them would have had no existence, and associated with Papists in an act of Parliament which deprived them of their civil rights, the most earnest of them abandoned the unthankful service; they saw at last that the liberties for which they and their fathers fought were not to be theirs in Ireland. If they intended to live as freemen, speaking no lies, and professing openly the creed of the Reformation they must seek a country where the long arm of Prelacy was still too short to reach them. During the first half of the eighteenth century, Down, Antrim, Tyrone, Armagh and Derry were emptied of Protestant inhabitants who were of more value to Ireland than Californian gold mines, while the scattered colonies of the South, *denied chapels of their own* and if they did not wish to be atheists or Papists, offered the alternative of conformity or departure, took the Government at their word and melted away.

During the turmoil following the Protestant Reformation in England it is recorded that the landed aristocracy of that country became Protestant or Catholic just as their profession of one faith or the other seemed necessary to save their estates. They were first Catholic, then turned Protestant with Henry VIII in order to share in the plunder of the rich estates of the Catholic Church, its monasteries, endowments, &c., and as monarch succeeded monarch the nobility changed their faith to suit that of the monarch, always stipulating however for the retention of their spoil.

In Ireland a somewhat similar phenomenon was witnessed at the later date with which we are dealing. The landed aristocracy amongst the Presbyterians did not withstand the persecutions but studied their comforts by renouncing their religion. The author of the *History of Irish Presbyterianism* says, and the saying is well corroborated elsewhere, that "the Presbyterian aristocracy had gone over to Prelacy which they had sworn to extinguish", and in another place he thus sums up the results of this upon the political situation of the Presbyterians, and he might have included all the sects outside of the Episcopal Church in the century immediately following the Battle of the Boyne:-

Presbyterians, having no political power, had to submit to political persecutions. The feudal system which transferred the ownership of the soil from the toiler to the landlord was one of the many evils introduced by the power of England. The Presbyterian farmer was a serf who had to submit to the will of his landlord, and in elections when he had a vote, to support the enemies of his creed, his class and his country.

The Test Acts which were responsible for much of this persecution of Protestants by Protestants in the name of religion were practically

20

abolished by the Irish Parliament under pressure by the armed Volunteers in 1780, but the iniquitous system of private ownership of land had already at that time borne bitter fruit to the Ulster Protestant farmers.

As the rank and file of the Protestant armies had been defrauded of the religious liberties for which they had fought, so also were they defrauded of their hopes of social or economic independence.

We have pointed out before, that the Ulster plantation of James I was a scheme under which the lands stolen from the natives were given to certain Crown favourites and London companies, and that the rank and file of the Protestant English and Scottish armies were only made tenants of these aristocrats and companies. Tyrone, Derry, Donegal, Fermanagh, Armagh and Cavan were entirely confiscated. The plan was worked out by Sir Arthur Chichester, ancestor of the Marquis of Donegal. For his share in the transaction he received the entire territories of the clansmen of Sir Cahir O'Doherty; the London companies, which had financed the war, received 209,800 acres out of a total of 500,000 acres, and other ancestors of the Orange aristocracy got the rest. In addition to the above-mentioned plunder, when Sir Arthur Chichester resigned his position as Lord Deputy in 1616, he received certain lands in Antrim and the title of Baron of Belfast.

All the Antrim lands were settled by a Protestant tenantry, the Catholics being driven to the hills and glens or allowed to remain on sufferance as labourers. As was natural from the political circumstances of the time, and in order to preserve the appearance of fairness, these Protestant tenants were at first granted very long leases. Under the security of tenure afforded by these leases, they worked hard, reclaimed the land, built houses, drained, fenced, and improved the property.

Also, under the terms of the promise given by William III, when in answer to the petition of the English woollen manufacturers he suppressed that industry in Ireland, but promised bounties to the linen industry as a compensation, the cultivation of flax and the manufacture of linen grew up in Antrim as a further contribution to the prosperity of the tenants of Lord Donegal.

But in and about the year 1772 the leases began to expire all over the country. What happened then is best told in the words of the *Remonstrance of Northern Protestants* sent to the Lord Lieutenant, Lord Townshend, in that year:−

The landlords thirsted to share the people's benefits by raising their rents which would have been very reasonable to a moderate degree, but of late they had run to great excesses.

When the tenant's lease was ended, they published in the newspapers that such a parcel of land was to be let, and that proposals in writing would be received for it. They invited every covetous, envious, and malicious person to offer for his neighbour's possessions and improvements. The tenant, knowing he must be the highest bidder, or turn out he knew not whither, would offer more than their value. If he complained to the landlord that it was too dear, the landlord answered that he knew it was, but that as it was in a trading country, the tenant could make up the deficiency by his industry.

Those who possessed the greatest estates were now so rich that they could not find delicacies enough in their own country to bestow their wealth on, but carried it abroad to lavish there the entire day's sweat of thousands of poor people.

The two worst extortioners were Lord Donegal and a Mr. Upton. On the estate of Lord Donegal a large number of the leases expired simultaneously. The landlord refused to renew them unless he received the enormous sum of £100,000 in fines as a free gift for his generosity. As the tenants could not raise this great sum they offered to pay the interest upon it in addition to their rent, but this was refused, and then some "hard-headed, shrewd and enterprising Belfast capitalists" offered the money to my lord and secured the farms over the head of the tenants, who were accordingly evicted. According to Froude, in his *English in Ireland in the Eighteenth Century* (and Froude was as bitter, malevolent and anti-Irish a historian as ever wrote), "In the two years that followed the Antrim evictions, thirty thousand Protestants left Ulster for a land where there was no legal robbery, and where those who sowed the seed could reap the harvest".

Those who remained at home did not accept their fate with complacency, nor show that voluntary abasement before the aristocracy characteristic of their descendants to-day. They formed a secret society – 'The Hearts of Steel' – which strove by acts of terrorism to redress some of their grievances. In a manifesto issued by this organisation in 1772 the following sentence appears:–

The Supreme Judge himself had excited them to commotion, to cause the landlords on whom no mild means will prevail to observe the pale faces and the thin clothing of their honest Protestant subjects who had enriched the country by their industry.

When in the same year six of their number were arrested and lodged in the town jail of Belfast, the members of this Society assembled from all parts of Down and Antrim, marched upon Belfast, stormed the jail, and released their comrades. The thin clothing and pale faces of honest Protestant workers are still in evidence in Belfast. Let us hope that they will ere long be marching again to storm the capitalist system which has for so long imprisoned not only the bodies but the souls of their class.

Chapter III

Dublin in the Twentieth Century

Someone has said that the most deplorable feature of Irish life is the apparent lack of civic consciousness. It is, indeed, strange that the people of a nation, which has shown indomitable determination in its struggle for the possession of the mere machinery of government, should exhibit so little capacity to breathe a civic soul into such portions of the machinery as they had already brought under their control. That this phenomenon is explicable in a manner not at all to the discredit of the citizens of the towns and cities of Ireland is quite true, but true also is it that a full and generous admission of the adverse influences that have hindered or retarded the development of a civic or municipal, as distinguished from an aggressive or even self-sacrificing national patriotism, does not absolve those citizens from the duty of labouring to overcome our national failing in this respect. An Irish municipality elected by the male and female voters under the present suffrage ought to be, in its public activities, breadth of outlook, and comprehensiveness of ambition for the social well-being and mental enrichment of its inhabitants, a centre of pride to the Irish race, and a shining example of the possibilities of the future of Ireland under free and self-governing institutions.

Its failure to do so, if it does fail, will not, indeed, vitiate the strength of the claim for national independence, but it will unquestionably weaken the powers making in that direction, as well as sadden the hearts of those who, amidst the struggles of to-day, require the mental aid to be derived from an idealising of the human elements with whom they are allied, and upon whom they hope to build the future.

An almost complete change in the intellectual view-point of the mass of the Irish people would be required to establish, in its proper place and relative importance, the modern conception of the function of public bodies as a governing factor in Irish municipal politics. It would necessitate such a change as would impel the public to regard such public bodies, not so much as offensive weapons to be won from a political enemy in order that he may be silenced, but rather as effective tools to be used in the up-building of a healthier social edifice in which to give effect to the needs of the citizens for associative aids to their individual development and culture.

This is, indeed, the needed point of view. We require in Ireland to grasp the fact that the act of voting at the ballot-box is the one act in which we get the opportunity to give expression to the soul of the race; the act in which we give a tangible body to our public spirit. The ballot-box is the vehicle of expression of our social consciousness; by means of it we collect all the passions, all the ideals, all the desires, all the ambitions, all the strengths, all the weaknesses, all the integrity, all the corruption, all the elevating aspirations, and all the debasing interests of the population, and make of them a composite whole which henceforth takes its place in history as the embodied soul of the race at that period of its development. A people are not to be judged by the performances of their great men, nor to be estimated spiritually by the intellectual conquests of their geniuses. A truer standard by which the spiritual and mental measurement of a people can be taken in modern times, is by the picture drawn of itself by itself when at the ballot-box, it surrenders the care of its collective destiny into the hands of its elected representatives.

The question whether such elected persons have or have not the power to realise the desires of their constituents scarcely enters into the matter. It is not by its power to realise high ideals a people will and must be judged, but by the standard of the ideals themselves. A people with high ideals of collective responsibility and public virtues it is politically impotent to realise, will necessarily rank higher in the scale of humanity than a people in full possession of political power, but destitute of public spirit and civic virtue.

Up to the passing of the Local Government (Ireland) Act of 1898 there existed no means by which the democracy of the Irish towns could be tested in order to ascertain the measure of their civic patriotism. The Local Government of Ireland was exclusively in the hands of the propertied class. The Municipal Councils outside of Belfast were elected on a restricted property qualification, and whatever evils existed in the urban districts were no more under the control of the mass of the people than if they had been resident in Timbuctoo or Terra-del-Fuego.

Indeed, by means of the Parliamentary franchise, the masses in the Irish cities could conceivably exert a determining influence on the fate of countries at the extremest limits of the earth, while unable to seriously affect the lighting or paving of the streets in which they lived. At such a time the propertied Irish patriot would occasionally refer to the unhealthy, squalid condition of Dublin, for example, as an evidence of the evils resulting from British rule; evils which would assuredly disappear before the beneficent hand of a popularly-elected Irish administration. Nor can we wonder at such a belief. Assuredly it was within the realm of probability, that a people suffering under the smart of intolerable conditions caused by a misuse of political power and social privilege should, at the first opportunity, set itself to the task of sweeping away such conditions by a public-spirited use of their newly-acquired control of municipal powers. The concept of the Irish nation as an organic whole, each part of which throbs in fullest sympathy with every other, and feels in the movements of its public administrative bodies, the pulsations of its own intellectual heart-beats, a concept vaguely outlined in the dreams of patriotic enthusiasts, poets and martyrs of the past, might reasonably have been expected to take form and substance in miniature, with the establishment of popular control over cities in which hundreds of thousands of Irish men, women and children passed their lives.

If it has not taken form; if to-day the cities and towns of Ireland are a reproach to the land and a glaring evidence of the incapacity of the municipal rulers of the country, the responsibility for the failure lies largely with those who, in the past, had control of the political education of the Irish masses, and failed to prepare them for the intelligent exercise of those public powers for which they were taught to clamour. That they were not prepared, and that no effort is therefore being made to give form and substance to any conception of civic patriotism, is only too evident to those who are even casually acquainted with the majority of Irish cities. A glance at the condition of Dublin, for instance, reveals a state of matters sadly eloquent of the woeful lack of public spirit in those who are responsible as municipal rulers, and those who, as electors, tolerate such rulers.

The following comment of *The Medical Press*, upon the occasion of the conferring of the Freedom of the City upon Sir Charles Cameron, gives in concise form the facts relative to the health of Dublin in 1911, and is useful also as an illustration of the opinion of enlightened outsiders upon our municipal progress, or lack of progress, and as a comparison with the cities usually reckoned the least progressive in the world:–

In the resolution conferring the freedom of the City on Sir Charles Cameron, says *The Medical Press*, it is stated that Dublin can now boast of comparative freedom from almost all of the malignant diseases which assail mankind.

If such a boast were made it would be a lying one. Again reference is made to the "excellent state of public health" which "now obtains in Dublin". Let us get to facts. According to the latest returns, the death-rate in Dublin was 27.6 per 1,000. This was the highest of any City in Europe, as given in the Registrar-General's list, the next highest being that of Moscow – 26.3 per 1,000. In Calcutta, in the presence of plague and cholera, the rate was only 27 per 1,000. Again, in the first six weeks of the present year, there were 63 deaths – ten a week – from four infectious diseases – scarlatina, typhoid, diphtheria and whooping-cough. Yet this epidemic is what an Alderman of the City – generally well-informed – airily described at a public dinner the other day as "trifling".

The thoughtful reader cannot but be impressed and saddened by the comparison drawn, in the above extract, between Dublin and such cities as Moscow and Calcutta. That it should be possible to draw such a comparison, or any comparison but a favourable one, between the capital of Ireland governed by its citizens and a city ruled autocratically by the liberty-hating officials of Russian Czardom is bad enough, but that an even more unfavourable comparison could truthfully be drawn between Dublin and an Asiatic city inhabited by a population destitute of civic power or political responsibility, and unacquainted with the first laws of hygienic teaching, is surely so much a humiliation that it should fire every Irishman and woman with a fierce eagerness to remove such a stigma. Lest some of our readers might think that the English source from which this extract is taken may possibly be unduly influenced by national prejudice in its criticism (a most unfair assumption), we may quote the declaration of the Medical Officer of Health in question in his remarkable *Letter to the Lord Mayor*(of Dublin) in 1909. The comparison he draws is even more useful, as the towns instanced possess the same municipal powers, and are elected upon the same franchise as Dublin. He says:–

It must be admitted that the general death-rate is far in excess of the mean death-rate in English towns.

In 1908 the mean death-rate in the 76 largest English towns was 15.8. The death-rate in the Dublin Registration Area was 21.5, the rate in the City being 23. The rate in the Metropolitan Area is that which in fairness should be compared with the English rates. The highest urban death-rate in England – namely, 19.8 – was in Oldham.

A comparison of these figures of Sir Charles Cameron with those cited in the first quotation, would seem to point to an actual increase in the death-rate of 1911 as compared with 1908. Viewed from another standpoint, the figures in both quotations prove the continued and needless sacrifice of life in Ireland. Accepting the English figures as the lowest at present obtainable in the present state of knowledge, and in the efficiency for social purposes of our political institutions in our present hands, it follows that there is permitted in Ireland a state of matters which involves, as its necessary result, the ceaseless slaughter of precious human life. Other figures quoted by Sir Charles Cameron seem to show that it is upon the poor that the main burden of such slaughter falls, as the death-rate is nicely proportioned to the special status of the inhabitants of Dublin. The higher the social status the lower the death-rate, and the lower the social status the higher the death-rate.

Thus, in the Annual Report for the year 1903 he gives the death-rate in Dublin according to the classes represented in the population as follows:–

	Per 1,000
Professional and Independent Classes	26.4
Middle Class	14.9
Artisan Class and Petty Shopkeepers	18.7
General Service Class and Inmates of Workhouses	32.6

In a still minuter analysis he gives the figures of child mortality amongst different classes of the population as follows:–

Professional and Independent Classes

Population	17,436
Deaths of children under 5 years	16
Proportion of deaths of children per 1,000 of the population of the class	0.9

Middle Class

Population	87,186
Deaths of children under 5 years	239
Proportion of children's deaths per 1,000 of the population of the class	2.7

Artisan Class and Petty Shopkeepers

Population	110,423
Deaths of children under 5 years	530
Ratio of those deaths per 1,000 of the population of the class	4.8

General Service Class and Inmates of Workhouses

Population	89,861
Deaths of children under 5 years	1,145
Ratio of the deaths of children per 1,000 of the population of the class	27.7

Thus we have a steady increase in the death-rate from its lowest point – amongst the professional or independent class to its highest point – amongst the street hawkers and casual labourers. This was for the year 1905.

A table showing the death-rate according to the four quarters of the year shows also that the number of deaths in Dublin is highest in the first three months – January, February and March – the winter months when the severity of the season makes its worst ravages amongst the poor, too enfeebled by hunger and cold to withstand its shocks.

Thus the high death-rate of Dublin is seen to be entirely due to economic causes, to rise and fall with economic classes. The rich of Dublin enjoy as long an immunity from death as do their kind elsewhere; it is the slaughter of Dublin's poor that gives the Irish metropolis its unenviable and hateful notoriety amongst civilised nations.

Now, what is the cause of this terrible state of matters, this hideous blot upon the Irish name? The original causes are many, but the one cause of its continuance is the lack of public spirit amongst the municipal rulers, and that again is only possible because of the want of proper training in democratic ideas amongst the mass of the electors. Democracy, as a reasoned-out faith, has not had in Ireland yet the proper political or social environment in which to grow; whatever democracy there is is instinctive and spontaneous, and is not the result of sound political teachings or the outcome of deep reflections upon the growth and development of social or political institutions. Usually the democrats of Ireland have been rebels against political tyranny; the necessity of keeping up the fight for the establishment of the political machinery through which Democracy might express itself, interfered with, and indeed destroyed, the possibility of developing as a theory or philosophical system those democratic principles which inspired the rebels personally. And as the fate of the rebels was generally an unhappy one, the masses of the people have had no opportunity of assimilating democratic thought except in the fitful flashes of political oratory, or the almost as ephemeral pamphleteering of our more brilliant revolutionists. This is indeed the only assignable reason why our working-class voters as a rule use so badly these rights for which so many of our bravest and noblest fought and toiled and agonised during the long dark night of our past.

In awakening the working class to a realisation of the necessity of using their votes for the purpose of social regeneration, to make the city in which they live be an aid to their individual uplifting and to their physical and moral strength, it should ever be borne in mind that the representative institutions of that city should, as we have already said, be an expression of the soul of the race, and that, as the soul directs the activities of the body in a clean or unclean direction, so shall our representative governing bodies make for or against clean living in clean habitations in a clean city.

It is well to remember that the Conquest never interfered with the right or power of the individual in Ireland to grow rich by betraying or surrendering the nation; it was only against the nation and those who had identified themselves with it that that Conquest was directed. Hence the reversal of the Conquest implies the assertion of the rights and powers of the community (city or nation) over against those of the individual. The Conquest was, in Irish politics, the victory of the capitalist conception of law and the functions of law – the Re-Conquest will be the victory of the working-class conception, the re-establishment of the power of the community over the conditions of life that assist or retard the development of the individual.

On the Statute Book to-day there are certain laws giving to the Dublin workers, through the Corporation, powers over the conditions of life in their city. These powers, if properly and relentlessly utilised, would go a long way towards remedying that fearful state of affairs already cited, and would also be in direct accord with the general movement to re-establish the true Irish nation. The Corporation has the power to close and demolish insanitary houses, unless they are put in a state to satisfy the Board of Health. It has the power to execute necessary repairs to tenement houses, and compel the owners to pay the expense, if these owners refuse to execute the repairs themselves. It has the power to make bye-laws governing tenement houses, and can thus enforce the efficient cleaning, lighting, renovating and building of such houses according to the most modern hygienic ideas. This, of itself, could be made sufficient to revolutionise completely the tenement house system in the city. It has the power to build houses, and any money it borrows for that purpose does not affect its legal credit or borrowing powers as a municipality. It has the power to acquire land for the purpose of creating cemeteries, and can thus put an end to the scandalous robbery of the poor practised by the Catholic Cemeteries' Committee at Glasnevin.

These powers it already has; but other powers are needed and must be demanded, if the workers of Dublin would make the most of their inheritance. As the further powers required for Dublin are also required for the rest of the country, it would be unwise to develop that portion of our plan now, before dealing with the evil state of matters with which we find ourselves confronted all over Ireland as a result of our political subjection and social disorganisation in the past.

We cannot close this chapter more fittingly than by quoting with our own comments the following extracts from an Editorial in *The Irish Times* (Dublin) of 18th February, 1914, upon the *Report of the Departmental Committee of Inquiry into the Housing of the Dublin Working Classes*. Part of the Report itself is also quoted in the Appendix:–

The Report of the Departmental Committee of Inquiry into the housing conditions of the Dublin working classes was laid on the table of the House of Commons on Monday night. It is a document of almost historic importance; every word of it should have been submitted without delay to those whom it chiefly concerns – namely, the ratepayers of Dublin. The Commissioners have done their work fearlessly and well. We cannot suppose that there is in existence a more startling or arresting Blue Book. The report is a terrible indictment of the social conditions and civic administration of Dublin. Most of us had supposed ourselves to be familiar with the melancholy statistics of the Dublin slums. We knew that Dublin has a far larger percentage of single-room tenements than any other city in the Kingdom. We did not know that nearly twenty-eight thousand of our fellow-citizens live in dwellings which even the Corporation admits to be unfit for human habitation. We had suspected the difficulty of decent living in the slums; this report proves the impossibility of it. Nearly a third of our population so live that from dawn to dark and from dark to dawn it is without cleanliness, privacy or self-respect. The sanitary conditions are revolting, even the ordinary standards of savage morality can hardly be maintained. To condemn a young child to an upbringing in the Dublin slums is to condemn it to physical degradation and to an appalling precocity in vice.

These four level-headed civil servants have drawn a picture hardly less lurid than the scenes of Dante's *Inferno*, and they give chapter and verse for every statement. It is a bitter reproach to Dublin that their report should go forth to the world; but it is a necessary and well-deserved reproach.

We are to blame, but the chief share of blame rests on the Corporation of Dublin. The report is perfectly fair to the Corporation. It gives it full credit for what it has done in the matter of housing schemes, and recognises the weight of its inherited embarrassments. But the Commissioners have been compelled to find that the Corporation is directly responsible for the worst evils of the tenement system. They tear to pieces the excuse so often presented to ourselves and other critics – that admitted defects could not be remedied without fresh legislation. The report finds that the Corporation has grossly abused and mismanaged its existing powers. It has utterly failed to enforce its sanitary authority under the Act of 1890. It has encouraged slum-ownership not merely by connivance but by example. The report finds that three members of the Corporation – Aldermen O'Reilly and Corrigan and Councillor Crozier – are returned in evidence as owning, or being interested in nine, nineteen and eighteen tenement houses respectively. Some of their property is classed as "third-class property". Ten other members of the Corporation own, or are interested in, tenement houses. The report exposes the scandal of the rebate system, which was designed to encourage and reward decent and conscientious management of tenement property. The Commissioners are of opinion that in the case of some of the members of the Corporation who own tenements, rebates have been improperly allowed. They criticise sharply the "dispensing powers" which Sir Charles Cameron has seen fit to exercise. The Corporation, by its slackness and inefficiency, is directly responsible for the creation of a number of owners who have little sense of their duty as landlords. The report finds that, if the Corporation had rightly administered its own laws, it would have prevented the influx into Dublin of that large volume of rural labour which has depressed wages and intensified the tragedy of the slums. The Corporation's policy has at once increased and demoralised the miserable army of slum workers. 'Larkinism', in so far as it is a revolt against intolerable conditions of life, is one of the by-products of our civic administration.

The last sentence in that Editorial is typical of the general attitude in Ireland towards the Labour movement. Observe that *The Irish Times* declares that Larkinism is a revolt against intolerable conditions, remember that even Mr. William Martin Murphy was moved to tell the Dublin Employers that it was their sweating wages and bad conditions that produced Larkinism, remember also that no one can be found to deny that the general effect of Larkinism has been to raise wages and improve conditions, and then consider that all those who admit these things have combined and are combining to down Larkinism, and to represent it generally as the incarnation of evil, and you have a picture of the turmoil caused in our distressful country by the spectacle of the labourer organising and preparing to take his own.

You have also a typical representation of the antagonism between theory and practice. In theory they admit that conditions were intolerable, and that Larkin was justified in making war upon them; in practice they unite to defend those conditions, and to destroy the man or woman who rebels against them. How true does Charles Mackay say of the rebel before his time:–

> Him shall the scorn and wrath of men
> Pursue with deadly aim;
> And malice, envy, spite and lies
> Shall desecrate his name!

31

Chapter IV

Labour in Dublin

Whilst there have been long available statistics of the high rents and poor housing of the Dublin working class, there have not been, and are not even now available, statistics of the wages and labour conditions of Dublin.

The information which might be supplied to the general public by such statistics has for the most part been left to be gathered piecemeal by the workers themselves, and to be applied piecemeal in an unconnected fashion as it became necessary to use it for purposes of organisation and agitation. Used in such fashion it was never collected into one co-ordinated whole, such for instance, as Mr. Rowntree has given us in his study of the East End of London. One reason for this neglect of the social conditions of Dublin has been that in Ireland everything connected with the question of poverty insensibly became identified with one side or the other in the political fight over the question of national government. The reform temperament, if I may use such a phrase, could not escape being drawn into the fight for political reform, and the conservative temperament quite as naturally became a pawn in the game of political reaction. Now, it is well to remember that a conservative temperament is not naturally allied to social abuses or industrial sweating, but may be, very often is, the most painstaking of all the elements making for the correction of such abuses within certain limits; it is also well to be clear upon the fact that a readiness to fight, or even to die for national freedom, might co-exist in the same person with a vehement support of industrial despotism or landlord tyranny. Thus it has happened that all the literary elements of society, those who might have been, under happier political circumstances, the champions of the down-trodden Irish wage labourer or the painstaking investigators of social conditions, were absorbed in other fields, and the working class left without any means of influencing outside public opinion. As a result, outside public opinion in Dublin gradually came to believe that poverty and its attendant miseries in a city were things outside of public interest, and not in the remotest degree connected with public duties or civic patriotism. Poverty and misery were, in short, looked upon as evils which might call for the exercise of private benevolence, but their causes were to be looked for solely in the lapses or weaknesses of individual men and women, and not in the temporary social arrangements of an ever-changing industrial order.

In this Dublin, with all this welter of high political ideals and low industrial practices, vaulting Imperialism and grovelling sweating, there arose the working-class agitator. First as the Socialist, analysing and dissecting the differences between the principles and practices of the local bosses of the political parties, drawing attention to the fact that wages were lower and rents higher in Dublin than in England, that railwaymen received in Ireland from five shillings to ten shillings per week less for the same work than they did in England, that municipal employees were similarly relatively underpaid, that in private employment the same thing was true, and that the Irish worker had fought everybody's battles but his own. That there was no law upon the Statute Book, no order of the Privy Council, and no proclamation of the Lord Lieutenant which compelled or sought to compel Irish employers to pay lower wages than were paid for similar work in England, or Irish house-owners to charge higher rents. That the argument about struggling Irish industries as opposed to wealthy English ones was being used to bolster up firms which had been so long established that their position was as secure as that of any English firm; and yet, sheltering behind this argument, they continued to pay sweating wages of the worst kind.

It was further insisted that as the Irish farmer had only succeeded in breaking the back of Irish landlordism by creating a public opinion which made allegiance to the farmer synonymous with allegiance to Ireland, which treated as a traitor to Ireland all those who acted against the interests of the farmer, so the Irish working class could in its turn only emancipate itself by acting resolutely upon the principle that the cause of Labour was the cause of Ireland, and that they who sought to perpetuate the enslavement and degradation of Labour were enemies of Ireland, and hence part and parcel of the system of oppression. That the Conquest of Ireland had meant the social and political servitude of the Irish masses and therefore the Re-Conquest of Ireland must mean the social as well as the political independence from servitude of every man, woman and child in Ireland. In other words, the common ownership of all Ireland by all the Irish.

In the soil thus prepared there came at a lucky moment the organisation of the Irish Transport and General Workers' Union. This Union has, from its inception, fought shy of all theorising or philosophising about history or tradition, but addressing itself directly to the work nearest its hand, has fought to raise the standard of labour conditions in Dublin to at least an approximation of decent human conditions. To do this it has used as its inspiring battle-cry, as the watchword of its members, as the key-word of its message, the affirmation that "An injury to one is the concern of all" – an affirmation which we all admire when we read of it as the enunciation of some Greek or Roman philosopher, but which we are now being asked to abhor when, translated into action, it appears in our midst as 'The Sympathetic Strike'. Writing without time to consult books, we remember that one of the Wise Men of old, when asked "What was the most Perfect State?" answered "That in which an injury to the meanest citizen was considered as an outrage upon the whole body". And the reply has come down the ages to us as the embodiment of wisdom. Is it an illustration of the conflict between our theories and our practice that the lowest paid, least educated body of workers are the only people in Ireland who try to live up to this ideal, and that this attempt of theirs should lead to their being branded as outlaws?

What is the sympathetic strike? It is the recognition by the Working Class of its essential unity, the manifestation in our daily industrial relations that our brother's fight is our fight, our sister's troubles are our troubles, that we are all members one of another. In practical operation it means that when any body of workers is in conflict with their employers, that all other workers should co-operate with them in attempting to bring that particular employer to reason by refusing to handle his goods. That, in fact, every employer who does not consent to treat his workpeople upon a civilised basis should be treated as an enemy of civilisation, and placed and kept outside the amenities and facilities offered by civilised communities. In other words, that he and his should be made 'tabu', treated as unclean, as 'tainted', and therefore likely to contaminate all others. The idea is not new. It is as old as humanity. Several historical examples will readily occur to the mind of the thoughtful reader. The *Vehmgerichte* of Germany of the Middle Ages, where the offending person had a stake driven into the ground opposite his door by orders of the secret tribunal; and from that moment was as completely cut off from his fellows as if he were on a raft in mid-ocean, is one instance. The boycott of Land League days is another. In that boycott the very journals and politicians who are denouncing the Irish Transport Union used a weapon which in its actual operations was more merciless, cruel and repulsive than any sympathetic strike has ever yet been. And even the Church, in its strength and struggles when it was able to command obedience to its decrees of excommunication, supplied history with a stern application of the same principle which for thoroughness we could never hope to equal. Such instances could be almost indefinitely multiplied. When the peasants of France rose in the *Jacquerie* against their feudal barons, did not the English nobles join in sympathetic action with those French barons against the peasantry, although at that moment the English were in France as invaders and despoilers of the territory of those same French feudal barons? When the English peasantry revolted against their masters, did not all English aristocrats join in sympathetic action to crush them? When the German peasantry rose during the Reformation, did not Catholic and Protestant aristocrats cease exterminating each other to join in a sympathetic attempt to exterminate the insurgents?

When, during the French Revolution, the French people overthrew kings and aristocrats, did not all the feudal lords and rulers of Europe take sympathetic action to restore the French monarchy, even although doing it involved throwing all industrial life in Europe into chaos and drenching a Continent with blood?

Historically, the sympathetic strike can find ample justification. But – and this point must be emphasised – it was not mere cool reasoning that gave it birth in Dublin. In that city it was born out of desperate necessity. Seeing all classes of semi-skilled labour in Dublin so wretchedly underpaid and so atrociously sweated, the Irish Transport and General Workers' Union taught them to stand together and help one another, and out of this advice the more perfect weapon has grown.

That the Labour Movement there has utilised it before elsewhere is due to the fact that in that city what is known as general or unskilled labour bears a greater proportion to the whole body of workers than elsewhere. And hence the workers are a more movable, fluctuating body, are more often, as individuals, engaged in totally dissimilar industries than in the English cities, where skilled trades absorb so great a proportion and keep them so long in the one class of industry.

Out of all this turmoil and fighting the Irish working-class movement has evolved, is evolving, amongst its members a higher conception of mutual life, a realisation of their duties to each other and to society at large; and are thus building for the future in a way that ought to gladden the hearts of all lovers of the race. In contrast to the narrow, restricted outlook of the capitalist class, and even of certain old-fashioned trade unionists, with their perpetual insistence upon 'rights', it insists, almost fiercely, that there are no rights without duties, and the first duty is to help one another. This is indeed revolutionary and disturbing, but not half as much as would be a practical following out of the moral precepts of Christianity.

Chapter V

Belfast and Its Problems

From a municipal point of view Belfast is a distinct improvement upon Dublin. Municipally, it can compare favourably with any similar city in Great Britain, and its industrial conditions are the product of modern industrial slavery and can be paralleled wherever capitalism flourishes. The things in which Belfast is peculiar are the skilful use by the master class of religious rallying cries which, long since forgotten elsewhere, are still potent to limit and weaken Labour here, and the pharisaical spirit of self-righteousness which enables unscrupulous sweaters of the poor, with one hand in the pocket of their workers, to raise the other hand to heaven and thank God that they are not as other men.

When, therefore, we say that Belfast is an improvement on Dublin from a municipal point of view we mean just exactly what we say, and nothing more, and would protest against more being read into our statement. The homes of the poor are better, house rent is lower, and the city is cleaner and healthier than Dublin.

Reasons for this comparatively favourable state of matters are many. Belfast, as the price of its surrender of its national soul, as the price of its hatred of national freedom, obtained every kind of legislative sanction it desired for its municipal activities; Dublin has been as consistently denied such facilities. Belfast has been enabled to spread as far beyond its original boundaries as it desired, and to include its wealthiest districts within its taxable area; Dublin is still (1913) confined to a district not much larger than it covered before the Union, and its wealthiest traders have had the aid of the law in keeping their residential districts outside of the city limits. Rathmines and Rathgar, for instance, are scandalous examples of areas inhabited by the wealthiest traders and merchants who enjoy all the facilities offered by the City of Dublin and bear none of its burdens. But the reader unfamiliar with the City of Dublin will appreciate this gross injustice better when we say that a penny tram fare will bring a traveller from Nelson's Pillar in the heart of the city into the portions of the suburbs of Dublin occupied by the gentry of Dublin, but outside of the City limits. A penny tram ride in Belfast is much longer than a penny tram ride in Dublin, but whereas the penny tram ride in Dublin will take you out of the taxable area of the city, a two-penny tram ride in Belfast will still leave you within the city boundaries; this necessarily makes Belfast, apart altogether from its greater manufactures, a wealthier city than Dublin and leaves a much larger sum available for municipal activities and progress generally. Its taxation is more justly spread.

One other contributing cause is to be found in the circumstance that the greater part of the buildings in the heart of Belfast were built upon land originally acquired at nominal rents upon very long leases, whereas Dublin in its centre is occupied by old houses originally occupied as town mansions by the rack-renting aristocracy, and when these gentry moved to London they, in pursuance of their rack-renting instincts, let the houses at the highest rents they could squeeze out of them. Such houses have been let and re-let with an increase of rent accompanying each fresh letting, until Dublin is now confronted with the curious fact that although the tenant who hires the rooms is horribly rack-rented, yet the landlord from whom he hires may have but a small margin to live upon between the rent he receives and the rent he pays to the landlord from whom he had hired, and so *ad infinitum*.

One of the first things a Labour Party in Dublin Corporation should do, is to demand the publication of the names of the several owners of house property in the city. Only by such publication, and the investigation necessarily preceding it, would the tangle of house-ownership in Dublin be cleared up and the way cleared up for drastic enforcement of sanitary laws.

Our readers will see that the difference between the municipality of Dublin and that of Belfast is the difference between an old city, inheriting accumulations of abuses and obstructed at every turn by a hostile legislature, and a new city aided by a friendly legislature and unexpectedly spreading over agricultural land lightly valued and cheaply rented by its owners.

But Belfast has its own problems to deal with. In some respects these problems are more difficult than any Dublin knows; in some respects the horrors of Belfast life are such as Dublin may pray to be saved from.

With Belfast, as with Dublin, there is little need to go beyond official returns for any statements of facts. Dr. Baillie, Medical Officer of Health for Belfast, has on many occasions in his Annual Report set down in his dry official way some statistics as to the pressure of the Capitalist system upon the Belfast workers, and these statistics, well considered, might well produce a crop of revolutionists in the Northern City.

In his official report for 1909, referring to the extraordinary number of premature births, Dr. Baillie remarks:–

The premature births were found to be most prevalent among women who worked in mills and factories, engaged in such work as the following – spinning, weaving, machining, tobacco-spinning and laundry work. Many of the women appear to be utterly unable for such work owing to the want of sufficient nourishment and suitable clothing, and being through stress of circumstances compelled to work up to the date of confinement, this would be accountable for many young and delicate children found by the Health Visitors.

Dealing with consumption and the efforts at its cure, he gives the following figures illustrating again how it is the poor who are the principal sufferers from this, as from all the other scourges of life in Ireland:–

As in the previous year, the class of persons most attacked were housewives (280), the next in order being labourers (179), mill-workers (162), children (117), warehouse workers (107), factory workers (59), and clerks (34).

Dr. Baillie further drives home the lesson of the cause of consumption when he says:–

The districts suffering most severely from this disease are Nos.3, 4 and 12, in which 136, 117 and 112 cases occurred respectively, and it is to be noted that in these districts textile industries are largely carried on.

Of the total number of cases (1,317) coming under the observation of this Department, 708 were females and 609 males, showing the number of females to be 99 in excess of that of males. This is somewhat different to that which is found in most other cities, and may be partially due to the nature of the work in which the female population is engaged.

As in previous years, it was found that consumption was most prevalent amongst the poor, owing largely to the unfavourable conditions under which necessity compels them to live – such as dark, ill-ventilated houses and insanitary habits, together with insufficient food and clothing.

This is confirmatory of the previous saying of Dr. Koch, of Berlin, that the chief cause of consumption was to be found in the unsanitary houses and workshops of the poor. The Socialist contention that most diseases could be eliminated by the establishment of a juster social order, and that the capitalist system is mainly responsible for sickness and the poverty that follows from sickness, as well as the sickness that follows from poverty, is thus strikingly verified from impartial sources.

Of Typhus Fever Dr. Baillie says, and the admission is remarkable, that:–

This disease is extremely proved to be associated with conditions of privation, poverty, and over-crowding, bad feeding and intemperance.

The disease in question does not claim many victims in Belfast, but it is interesting to notice that this medical gentleman places the responsibility for the disease upon the proper shoulders, those responsible for bad social conditions – a fact to be commended to the notice of those good souls who, when they see their children, parents, sisters or brothers murdered by disease, blasphemously attribute their deaths to the 'Will of God'. It is not to the Will of God, but to the greed of man that most such deaths are due.

To those who are acquainted, even on hear-say, with the conditions in the mills of Belfast, it will be no surprise to learn that the poor are the chief sufferers from consumption and especially the poor mill-workers. Imagine a spinning-room so hot with a moist heat that all girls and women must work in bare feet, with dress open at breast and arms bare, hair tied up tight to prevent it irritating the skin rendered irritable and tender by sweat and heat; imagine the stifling, suffocating atmosphere that in a few months banishes the colour from the cheeks of the rosiest half-timer and reduces all to one common deadly pallor; imagine all the windows closed in such a place, or only opened for a few minutes when the advent of the Lady (Factory) Inspector is announced, and closed immediately she retires; imagine all the machinery driven at ever increasing speed in such an inferno, and imagine these poor slaves at meal hours catching up their shawls and rushing out, perhaps amid rain or frost, to snatch up a few badly-cooked mouthfuls of badly nourishing food and be back in their places inside of 45 minutes! Is it any wonder that such people, working amid such conditions, are subject to consumption? The medical authorities issue long and minute instructions to the people as to how consumption may be avoided, but the instructions are as a rule utterly valueless to the class most subject to the scourge. Of what use is it to teach people about the evil of overcrowding when their wages will not permit them to secure decent house room? Of what avail a paper telling how to cook and prepare food when they have only 45 minutes to come from the mill, cook a meal, eat it, and return to the mill – the mother being one of the bread-winners or wage-earners of the family? Of what avail instilling into the worker the necessity of choosing proper food to counteract the tendency to consumption, and so increase the resisting power of the individual, when the wages are so small that only the poorest, easiest cooked, and generally least nutritious foods can be bought?

We do not deny the benevolent motives of the good ladies and gentlemen at present crusading against consumption in Ireland, but we consider that the agitator who aroused the people to revolt against the conditions of toil and life for the workers is doing more to end the scourge than all the anti-tuberculosis societies ever dreamed of. Consider, for instance, the life of the sweated home-workers of Belfast, and imagine what poor resisting power their bodily frames must offer to the inroads of the White Plague. We quote again from Dr. Baillie:–

In the last week in December, for instance, a woman was observed embroidering small dots on cushion covers, there were 308 dots on each cushion, and for sewing these by hand she received the sum of one penny. She said that for a day's work of that kind she would have difficulty in making sixpence. Nor is this an exceptional case. Quite recently our inspector was shown handkerchiefs which were to be ornamented by a design in dots; these dots were counted and it was found that the worker had to sew 384 dots for one penny. Comment is needless; other classes of work are as badly paid. The finishing of shirts, which consists of making buttonholes, sewing on buttons and making small gussets at the wrists and sides of the shirts, may be instanced. In each, six or seven buttonholes have to be cut or hand-sewn, eight buttons have to be sewn on, and four gussets made. This work is paid at the rate of sixpence for one dozen shirts. Nor is this a cheap class of goods, permitting scamped work. The sewing has to be neat and well-finished, and the buttonholes evenly sewn, the shirts being of a fine quality for which the buying public has to give a good price.

The making-up trades in general pay very poorly, among the various kinds of badly paid work noticed may be mentioned children's pinafores, flounced and braided at 4½d. per dozen, women's chemises at 7½ d. per dozen, women's aprons at 2½d. per dozen, men's drawers at 10d. per dozen, men's shirts at 10d. per dozen, blouses at 9d. per dozen, and babies' overalls at 9d. per dozen. From these very low rates of pay must be deducted the time spent in visiting the warerooms for work, the necessary upkeep of the worker's sewing machine, and the price of thread used in sewing, which is almost invariably provided by the worker.

One penny per hour is the ordinary rate of pay, and in many instances it falls below this.

In these industrial parts of the North of Ireland the yoke of capitalism lies heavy upon the lives of the people. The squalor and listless wretchedness of some other parts is, indeed, absent, but in its stead there exists grinding toil for old and young – toil to which the child is given up whilst its limbs and brains are still immature and undeveloped, and toil continued until, a broken and enfeebled wreck, the toiler sinks into a too early grave. In this part of Ireland the child is old before it knows what it is to be young. We have heard of a savage chief who was brought from his savage home to see and be impressed with the works of civilisation. He was taken around the big centres of modern capitalism, shown steam engines, battleships, guns, railway trains, big factories and churches, and all the mammoth achievements of our day,

41

and then taken home to his people. Arrived there he was asked by his escort what he conceived to be the most wonderful thing he had seen, what had impressed him most, and he answered:–

"Little Children Working".

This thing which seemed so strange to the savage, who amid his savage surroundings, handicapped by lack of knowledge, and all its industrial possibilities, yet had never thought of making children work, this thing is the great outstanding feature of life in Belfast and the industrial parts of Ireland. In their wisdom our lords and masters often leave full-grown men unemployed, but they can always find a use for the bodies and limbs of our children. A strange comment upon the absurdities of the capitalist system, illustrating its idiotic wastefulness of human possibilities; that the intellect and strength of men should be left to rot for want of work, whilst children are by premature work deprived of the possibilities of developing fully their minds or bodies.

Nor is this the only manner in which the life of the working class is sacrificed to the greed of dividends. Our shipyards offer up a daily sacrifice of life and limb on the altar of capitalism. The clang of the ambulance bell is one of the most familiar daily sounds on the streets between our shipyards and our hospitals.

It has been computed that some seventeen lives were lost on the *Titanic* before she left the Lagan; a list of the maimed and hurt and of those suffering from minor injuries, as a result of the accidents at any one of those big ships would read like a roster of the wounded after a battle upon the Indian frontier. The public reads and passes on, but fails to comprehend the totality of suffering involved. But it all means lives ruined, fair prospects blighted, homes devastated, crippled wrecks of manhood upon the streets, or widows and orphans to eat the bread of poverty and pauperism.

Add to this an army of insurance doctors paid, to belittle the injury, and declare the injured to be well and hearty, a host of lawyers whose practice depends upon their success in confusing honest workers when endeavouring, amid unfamiliar surroundings, to tell the truth about the mangling or killing of their workmates, and, finally, a hostile judge treating every applicant for just compensation as if they were known and habitual criminals, and you have a faint idea of one side of industrial life (and death) in the North of Ireland.

It is not so easy with accidents as it is with diseases to make the public realise that they are mostly *preventable*, yet that this is the case is susceptible of proof to the unbiassed mind. Even many workers will pooh-pooh the idea, accustomed as they have been to seeing accidents almost every day of their working lives, yet a little calm reflection will convince all but the most obdurate that an alteration of working conditions could be made which would go far to minimise the dangers of even the most perilous of our occupations.

Competent investigators, for instance, have found that the greatest number of accidents occur at two specific periods of the working day – viz., in the early morning and just before stopping work at evening. In the early morning when the worker is still drowsy from being aroused too early from his slumbers, and has not had time to settle down properly to his routine of watchfulness and alertness, or, as the homely saying has it, "whilst the sleep is still in his bones", the toll of accidents is always a heavy one.

After 9 a.m. they become less frequent and continue so until an hour after dinner. Then they commence again and go on increasing in frequency as the workers get tired and exhausted, until they rise to the highest number in the hour or half-hour immediately before ceasing work. How often do we hear the exclamation apropos of some accident involving the death of a worker: "He had only just started", or "he had only ten minutes to go before stopping for the day"? And yet the significance of the fact is lost on most.

Were these industries owned in common by the community and conducted for the benefit of all instead of for the private profit of a few capitalists, care would be taken that the working hours were not at any time so prolonged as to weary the worker and thus destroy his vigour and alertness; and, when an accident did occur, the persons in charge would be placed upon trial and compelled to prove their innocence of responsibility, instead of, as at present, when the friends of the victim are compelled to establish the responsibility of the employer, and can only establish it by the evidence of workers whose daily bread is at the mercy of the employer in question. But pending that desirable outcome of the Labour Movement, the efforts of the workers upon the industrial and political field should seek amongst other things:–

The abolition of the early morning start.

The abolition of all task or piecework or 'rushing' systems – red with the blood of the workers.

Reduction of the working day to the limit of eight hours or less, forbidding the physical and mental exhaustion of the workers.

Compensation for accidents to equal full pay of the worker injured.

Pensions to all widows of workers killed at work, such pensions to be a charge upon the firm employing the worker; onus of collecting and disbursing said pension to lie upon the State.

The majority of the poor slaves who work under such conditions and for such pay, as also the majority of the mill and factory workers amongst whom consumption claims its most numerous victims are, in Belfast, descendants of the men who "fought for civil and religious liberty at Derry, Aughrim and the Boyne".

If those poor sweated descendants of Protestant rebels against a king had to-day one-hundredth part of the spirit of their ancestors in question, the re-conquest of Ireland by the working class would be a much easier task than it is likely to prove.

But into the minds of the wisest of both sections there is gradually percolating the great truth that our common sufferings provide a common basis of action – an amalgam to fuse us all together, and that, as we suffer together we should fight together, that we may be free together. Thus out of our toil and moil there arises a new Party – the Party of Labour – to

> Tell of the cause of the poor who shrink
> Crushed grapes in the wine press,
> While rich men drink
> And barter the trodden wine,
> And pray.

Chapter VI

Woman

In our chapter dealing with the industrial conditions of Belfast, it was noted that the extremely high rate of sickness in the textile industry, the prevalence of tuberculosis and cognate diseases, affected principally the female workers, as does also the prevalence of a comparative illiteracy amongst the lower-paid grades of Labour in that city.

The recent dispute in Dublin also brought out in a very striking manner the terrible nature of the conditions under which women and girls labour in the capital city, the shocking insanitary conditions of the workshops, the grinding tyranny of those in charge, and the alarmingly low vitality which resulted from the inability to procure proper food and clothes with the meagre wages paid. Consideration of such facts inevitably leads to reflection on the whole position of women in modern Ireland, and their probable attitude towards any such change as that we are forecasting.

It will be observed by the thoughtful reader, that the development in Ireland of what is known as the women's movement has synchronised with the appearance of women upon the industrial field, and that the acuteness and fierceness of the women's war has kept even pace with the spread amongst educated women of a knowledge of the sordid and cruel nature of the lot of their suffering sisters of the wage-earning class.

We might say that the development of what, for want of a better name, is known as sex-consciousness, has waited for the spread amongst the more favoured women, of a deep feeling of social consciousness, what we have elsewhere in this work described as a civic conscience. The awakening amongst women of a realisation of the fact that modern society was founded upon force and injustice, that the highest honours of society have no relation to the merits of the recipients, and that acute human sympathies were rather hindrances than helps in the world, was a phenomenon due to the spread of industrialism and to the merciless struggle for existence which it imposes.

45

Upon woman, as the weaker physical vessel, and as the most untrained recruit, that struggle was inevitably the most cruel; it is a matter for deep thankfulness that the more intellectual women broke out into revolt against the anomaly of being compelled to bear all the worst burdens of the struggle, and yet be denied even the few political rights enjoyed by the male portion of their fellow-sufferers.

Had the boon of political equality been granted as readily as political wisdom should have dictated, much of the revolutionary value of woman's enfranchisement would probably have been lost. But the delay, the politicians' breach of faith with the women, a breach of which all parties were equally culpable, the long-continued struggle, the ever-spreading wave of martyrdom of the militant women of Great Britain and Ireland, and the spread amongst the active spirits of the Labour movement of an appreciation of the genuineness of the women's longings for freedom, as of their courage in fighting for it, produced an almost incalculable effect for good upon the relations between the two movements.

In Ireland the women's cause is felt by all Labour men and women as their cause; the Labour cause has no more earnest and whole-hearted supporters than the militant women. Rebellion, even in thought, produces a mental atmosphere of its own; the mental atmosphere the women's rebellion produced, opened their eyes and trained their minds to an understanding of the effects upon their sex of a social system in which the weakest must inevitably go to the wall, and when a further study of the capitalist system taught them that the term 'the weakest' means in practice the most scrupulous, the gentlest, the most humane, the most loving and compassionate, the most honourable, and the most sympathetic, then the militant women could not fail to see, that capitalism penalised in human beings just those characteristics of which women supposed themselves to be the most complete embodiment. Thus the spread of industrialism makes for the awakening of a social consciousness, awakes in women a feeling of self-pity as the greatest sufferers under social and political injustice; the divine wrath aroused when that self-pity is met with a sneer, and justice is denied, leads women to revolt, and revolt places women in comradeship and equality with all the finer souls whose life is given to warfare against established iniquities.

The worker is the slave of capitalist society, the female worker is the slave of that slave. In Ireland that female worker has hitherto exhibited, in her martyrdom, an almost damnable patience. She has toiled on the farms from her earliest childhood, attaining usually to the age of ripe womanhood without ever being vouchsafed the right to claim as her own a single penny of the money earned by her labour, and knowing that all her toil and privation would not earn her that right to the farm which would go without question to the most worthless member of the family, if that member chanced to be the eldest son.

The daughters of the Irish peasantry have been the cheapest slaves in existence – slaves to their own family, who were, in turn, slaves to all social parasites of a landlord and gombeen-ridden community. The peasant, in whom centuries of servitude and hunger had bred a fierce craving for money, usually regarded his daughters as beings sent by God to lighten his burden through life, and too often the same point of view was as fiercely insisted upon by the clergymen of all denominations. Never did the idea seem to enter the Irish peasant's mind, or be taught by his religious teachers, that each generation should pay to its successors the debt it owes to its forerunners; that thus, by spending itself for the benefit of its children, the human race ensures the progressive development of all. The Irish peasant, in too many cases, treated his daughters in much the same manner as he regarded a plough or a spade – as tools with which to work the farm. The whole mental outlook, the entire moral atmosphere of the countryside, enforced this point of view. In every chapel, church or meeting-house the insistence was ever upon duties – duties to those in superior stations, duties to the Church, duties to the parents. Never were the ears of the young polluted (?) by any reference to 'rights', and, growing up in this atmosphere, the women of Ireland accepted their position of social inferiority. That, in spite of this, they have ever proven valuable assets in every progressive movement in Ireland, is evidence of the great value their co-operation will be, when to their self-sacrificing acceptance of duty they begin to unite its necessary counterpoise, a high-minded assertion of rights.

We are not speaking here of rights, in the thin and attenuated meaning of the term to which we have been accustomed by the Liberal or other spokesmen of the capitalist class, that class to whom the assertion of rights has ever been the last word of human wisdom. We are rather using it in the sense in which it is used by, and is familiar to, the Labour movement.

We believe, with that movement, that the serene performance of duty, combined with and inseparable from the fearless assertion of rights, unite to make the highest expression of the human soul. That soul is the grandest which most unquestionably acquiesces in the performance of duty, and most unflinchingly claims its rights, even against a world in arms. In Ireland the soul of womanhood has been trained for centuries to surrender its rights, and as a consequence the race has lost its chief capacity to withstand assaults from without, and demoralisation from within. Those who preached to Irish womankind fidelity to duty as the only ideal to be striven after, were, consciously or unconsciously, fashioning a slave mentality, which the Irish mothers had perforce to transmit to the Irish child.

The militant women who, without abandoning their fidelity to duty, are yet teaching their sisters to assert their rights, are re-establishing a sane and perfect balance that makes more possible a well-ordered Irish nation.

47

The system of private capitalist property in Ireland, as in other countries, has given birth to the law of primogeniture under which the eldest son usurps the ownership of all property to the exclusion of the females of the family. Rooted in a property system founded upon force, this iniquitous law was unknown to the older social system of ancient Erin, and, in its actual workings out in modern Erin, it has been and is responsible for the moral murder of countless virtuous Irish maidens. It has meant that, in the continual dispersion of Irish families, the first to go was not the eldest son, as most capable of bearing the burden and heat of a struggle in a foreign country, but was rather the younger and least capable sons, or the gentler and softer daughters. Gentle Charles Kickham sang:–

> O brave, brave Irish girls,
> We well might call you brave;
> Sure the least of all your perils
> Is the stormy ocean wave.

Everyone acquainted with the lot encountered by Irish emigrant girls in the great cities of England or America, the hardships they had to undergo, the temptations to which they were subject, and the extraordinary proportion of them that succumbed to these temptations, must acknowledge that the poetic insight of Kickham correctly appreciated the gravity of the perils that awaited them. It is humiliating to have to record that the overwhelming majority of those girls were sent out upon a conscienceless world, absolutely destitute of training and preparation, and relying solely upon their physical strength and intelligence to carry them safely through. Laws made by men shut them out of all hope of inheritance in their native land; their male relatives exploited their labour and returned them never a penny as reward, and finally, when at last their labour could not wring sufficient from the meagre soil to satisfy the exactions of all, these girls were incontinently packed off across the ocean with, as a parting blessing, the adjuration to be sure and send some money home. Those who prate glibly about the 'sacredness of the home' and the 'sanctity of the family circle' would do well to consider what home in Ireland to-day is sacred from the influence of the greedy mercenary spirit, born of the system of capitalist property; what family circle is unbroken by the emigration of its most gentle and loving ones.

Just as the present system in Ireland has made cheap slaves or untrained emigrants of the flower of our peasant women, so it has darkened the lives and starved the intellect of the female operatives in mills, shops and factories. Wherever there is a great demand for female labour, as in Belfast, we find that the woman tends to become the chief support of the house. Driven out to work at the earliest possible age, she remains fettered to her wage-earning – a slave for life. Marriage does not mean for her a rest from outside labour, it usually means that, to the outside labour, she has added the duty of a double domestic toil. Throughout her life she remains a wage-earner; completing each day's work, she becomes the slave of the domestic needs of her family; and when at night she drops wearied upon her bed, it is with the knowledge that at the earliest morn she must find her way again into the service of the capitalist, and at the end of that coming day's service for him hasten homeward again for another round of domestic drudgery. So her whole life runs – a dreary pilgrimage from one drudgery to another; the coming of children but serving as milestones in her journey to signalise fresh increases to her burdens. Overworked, underpaid, and scantily nourished because underpaid, she falls easy prey to all the diseases that infect the badly-constructed 'warrens of the poor'. Her life is darkened from the outset by poverty, and the drudgery to which poverty is born, and the starvation of the intellect follows as an inevitable result upon the too early drudgery of the body.

Of what use to such sufferers can be the re-establishment of any form of Irish State if it does not embody the emancipation of womanhood. As we have shown, the whole spirit and practice of modern Ireland, as it expresses itself through its pastors and masters, bear socially and politically, hardly upon women. That spirit and that practice had their origins in the establishment in this country of a social and political order based upon the private ownership of property, as against the older order based upon the common ownership of a related community.

Whatever class rules industrially will rule politically, and impose upon the community in general the beliefs, customs and ideas most suitable to the perpetuation of its rule. These beliefs, customs, ideas become then the highest expression of morality and so remain until the ascent to power of another ruling industrial class establishes a new morality. In Ireland since the Conquest, the landlord-capitalist class has ruled; the beliefs, customs, ideas of Ireland are the embodiment of the slave morality we inherited from those who accepted that rule in one or other of its forms; the subjection of women was an integral part of that rule.

Unless women were kept in subjection, and their rights denied, there was no guarantee that field would be added unto field in the patrimony of the family, or that wealth would accumulate even although men should decay. So, down from the landlord to the tenant or peasant proprietor, from the monopolist to the small business man eager to be a monopolist, and from all above to all below, filtered the beliefs, customs, ideas establishing a slave morality which enforces the subjection of women as the standard morality of the country.

None so fitted to break the chains as they who wear them, none so well equipped to decide what is a fetter. In its march towards freedom, the working class of Ireland must cheer on the efforts of those women who, feeling on their souls and bodies the fetters of the ages, have arisen to strike them off, and cheer all the louder if in its hatred of thraldom and passion for freedom the women's army forges ahead of the militant army of Labour.

But whosoever carries the outworks of the citadel of oppression, the working class alone can raze it to the ground.

Chapter VII

Schools and Scholars of Erin

Ireland of old was styled the 'Land of saints and scholars'. It would be an ungrateful and thankless task to inquire to-day what proportion of saints she is able to rear upon her shores after seven centuries of British civilisation, and a century and a half of Anglo-Irish capitalism. Under such conditions saints do not grow in any noticeable numbers, and except in the homes of the poor, where patient self-denying mothers pinch and starve themselves in order to rear their families, or in workshops where women and girls toil at starvation wages that they may be able to keep from the door the wolf of want, and its still more ferocious companion, the hyena of temptation, the saints of latter-day Erin do not seem to exercise a very appreciable influence upon her social life. Certainly the latter-day minstrelsy and oratory of Erin seeks first for their subjects of eulogy, not Erin's saints but her politicians – a fact that is in itself a sufficient commentary upon the present outlook of the Irish people upon the importance of saintship.

But if it is difficult, if not impossible, to trace the saints of modern Erin, it is not impossible, nor even extraordinarily difficult, to understand the provision made for the production of scholars. And as we are considering the material left in Ireland, or shaping itself in Ireland for the re-conquest of Ireland and the establishment here of a social and political system guaranteeing freedom, and opportunities of development for all, it is incumbent upon us to consider what provision is now made for the physical and intellectual growth of the Irish workers – these workers who have to bear the burden of the present system, and whose children will have to build and shape the future.

Latter-day investigators have set beyond all doubt the truth that in Ancient Erin the chief and clan held in most repute were they who most esteemed and fostered the schools for the teaching of the wisdom of the day; and that even long after the Norman invasion the Irish schools and scholars continued to shed a lustre upon Gaelic civilisation, and to redeem Erin from the imputations her would-be masters so persistently strove to cast upon her native life. But with the consummation of the Conquest already noticed in these pages, the education of the Irish became an offence against the law, a price was put upon the head of a schoolmaster and he was hunted as eagerly as the wolf and the priest. Still the hunger for learning persisted, and overcame in many cases the evil laws and penalising decrees of the conquerors, and on lone mountain sides, in the midst of almost trackless bogs, and at the back of hedges, Irish boys and girls strove to snatch, illegally, the education denied them by their masters. Needless to say, however, under such conditions, education could not be universal; it was, on the contrary, only the few who could snatch some crumbs of learning in the midst of difficulties so appalling. Upon the great majority such conditions necessarily imposed ignorance as an inevitable result. For the Protestant minority schools were provided, by private enterprise and with the encouragement of the Government, but without any systematic oversight and regulations, and indeed with occasional lapses into irregularities almost unthinkable to the modern mind. A historical instance of this kind formed the subject of a fierce discussion in the Dublin House of Commons of 1790, during the term of what is known as Grattan's Parliament. There was then in Dublin a Foundling Hospital to which children from all parts of Ireland were sent by zealous philanthropists, and by many zealous people who were not philanthropists. Protestant orphans and Catholic children, whose parents had been tempted by hunger to surrender them to proselytisers, that they might not die of hunger before their eyes, were continually being despatched to this Foundling Hospital. The unhappy fate of these poor Irish waifs was thus told in Parliament by Sir John Blaquiere:–

The number of infants received in 1789 was 2,180, and of that number 2,087 were dead or unaccounted for. In ten years 19,367 children had been entered upon the books, and almost 17,000 were dead or missing. The wretched little ones were sent up from all parts of Ireland, ten or twelve of them thrown together in a kish or basket, forwarded in a low-backed car, and so bruised and crushed and shaken at their journey's end that half of them were taken out dead, and were flung into a dung-heap.

That last touch "flung into the dung-heap" is characteristic of the thought and practices of the ruling class of the time. The children were only children of the poor, and the poor – whether Protestant or Catholic – were only esteemed, perhaps are only esteemed to-day, by the rich, as in Kropotkin's words, "mere dung to manure the pasture lands of the rich expropriator".

Such scandals as the above were, of course, in their concentrated awfulness, exceptional, but in a very real sense it was typical of the abuse that followed inevitably upon the political and social system of the day. A Government based upon property, and denying the rights of the common people, must produce an administration of society which, in all its ramifications, will embody injustice. Brilliance of intellect it may have, great genius it may show, rare fruits in philosophy, art, science will blossom out of it, but, without democracy, it will remain a torture-house for the labourer, a prison for the hearts and hopes of the poor.

Between the institutions such as we have quoted amongst the Protestant minority, the illegal, but secretly tolerated, schools of the Catholics of the same period, and the National Schools of to-day, there stretches a great period of time – a period marked by many and far-reaching changes in the political situation. But in our treatment of the schools for our Irish children there is not to be observed any such radical or fundamental change as the development of the democracy would seem to warrant. On the contrary, that seems to be the one ground from which the public guardianship and responsibility, welcomed elsewhere, are here most resolutely forbidden to enter. Public responsibility, indeed, is admitted in a half-hearted form, but the right of control, of guardianship that goes, or should go, with responsibility is bluntly denied, and its assertion treated as a veritable attack upon the basis of public morality. Hence we do not find that the progress to be noted in other branches of public life is to be found here. The National Schools of Ireland have ever been left in the rear of progress, a menace to the health of the pupils and teachers, unsightly and dangerous products of a low standard of civic conscience.

A few quotations from impartial authorities upon the points we have noted will serve to illustrate how, in our own generation, the administration of schools still retains more than a flavour of the bad old anti-democratic days, with its contempt for the poor.

In the year 1900 *The Lancet* sent a Commissioner to investigate the sanitary conditions of the National Schools of Dublin. Of one of the schools he wrote:–

Schoolrooms dark and ill-ventilated; gas burning in the daytime; no recreation ground; no break from ten till two o'clock; no lavatory for the boys; manure heaps against walls of schools; dark brown liquid manure oozing from it forming stagnant pools, saturating unpaved porous ground; emanations from school garbage, dust heaps, black mud, fish heads, offal, &c., in the lanes and yards about.

In the year 1904 the Medical Officer of Health of the City of Dublin ordered his Sanitary Inspectors to investigate the sanitary conditions of the National Schools. Their report was embodied in his *Report of the State of Public Health* for that year, and shows that the general sanitary condition of the city schools was truly deplorable. When it is remembered that habits of cleanliness or uncleanliness contracted in childhood tend to root themselves in our natures, it will be understood how great an influence for evil such a school environment must have been to the children unfortunate enough to have been subjected to them. Such reflections will help to explain the deplorable apathy of many of the tenants of the Dublin slums, and their heart-breaking acquiescence in the continuance of conditions so destructive of the possibility of clean living. The report in question states that the English Board of Education requirements in the line of sanitary accommodation for schools, and the detailed reports of the Dublin inspectors show, that the Dublin schools seldom reach one-half of the standard necessary in the interests of health and decency. In some schools, for instance, St. Patrick's, Lower Tyrone Street, attended by 144 pupils, boys and girls, the w.c.'s were open to and used indiscriminately by boys and girls alike. We believe this school is now being demolished, it is to be trusted that the majority of its fellows will soon share the same fate.

In the same year as that in which *The Lancet* Commissioner reported on Dublin, a report to the Commissioners of National Education in Ireland dealing with Belfast, states of the schools in Newtownards district:–

After what has been said of the character of many of the houses and premises, it is not to be wondered at if sickness prevails to a large extent and epidemics spread rapidly. Ballymacarrett District is low-lying, and not an easy place to drain thoroughly, but the school-houses, no doubt, help the work of disease. I can count up fourteen monitors who have retired through ill-health, and have, I imagine, all since died. Two young monitresses employed in an overcrowded school have died within little more than a year.

Nine years afterwards, the Inspector for Belfast No.1 District was constrained to say in his Report to the same Commissioners upon the same subject:–

It is a pity, where so many agencies are at work making for the health of the people, that little children almost at the threshold of existence should be thrust into over-crowded rooms *where their young blood is slowly poisoned*.

How great this overcrowding is, and how bad its effects upon the health of the children, as well as upon their ability to benefit by the education provided, may be surmised by the following excerpts from the above-quoted Reports for the year 1909-10. Mr. Keith, the inspector, declared:–

Serious cases of overcrowding continue to occur. One city school supplies space for 291 children. At one visit I found 386 present. In one of the rooms, with accommodation for 47, 107 infants spend their school-days. At another school, where there is accommodation for 232, 324 children were in attendance, whilst 73 pupils were taught in a room for 44 and 116 in a room for 47. Part of the time, about 50 of the 116 referred to were taught in a tiled unheated passage, and this occurred on a snowy day in winter ... In another school 103 children were given a conversational lesson in a room 16 feet by 15 feet, accommodation 24. In this room 49 babies spent their school-days ... At another infants' school an unheated room 10 feet by 10 feet is used as a class-room. There the children have to endure one of two evils in the winter, either to perish with cold if the door is left open, or to inhale vitiated air if it is shut.

On visiting a school in September last, I found 37 pupils (boys and girls) under instruction in a small yard. Sixteen boys were sitting on the tiled floor of the yard, and two others were sitting with their backs to the door of one of the out-offices. The teacher thought this preferable to crowding the children into a class-room that is no better than a den.

The Report cites 43 schools in which the numbers present are always grossly in excess of the accommodation. The figures for the first ten will suffice:

	Accommodation	Present
1	18	53
2	34	130
3	50	115
4	6	33
5	47	151
6	50	145
7	23	43
8	17	52
9	29	74
10	21	42

The bearing of the capitalist system upon the problem of educating the young is shown in this statement of the Belfast Inspector:–

The cost of sites is a difficulty to be reckoned with in Belfast. I was informed that a rood of inferior building ground cost the promoters of a school about £500.

Five hundred pounds to be paid before Belfast can secure a rood 'of inferior building ground', upon which to erect a school to educate its children; and the landowners, who exact this tax upon enlightenment, are the political leaders of the people whose children's education they obstruct. One is inclined to wonder if it is only greed that impels the landed classes of Ulster to make such demands, when asked to provide land for educational purposes, or has the fear of educating the masses nothing to do with it? In two reports we find the attitude of the richer classes of Belfast thus strongly commented upon and condemned. In 1909-10:–

Again, the well-to-do classes in Belfast take very little interest in the schools ... The condition of many of the schools presents a powerful contrast to the phenomenal progress made by the city in so many directions.

In 1911-12:–

It is a pity that a city, in many respects so progressive, with "pride in its port and defiance in its eye", should have to look calmly on, while its children are either cooped-up in ill-ventilated class-rooms or left to face the perils of the streets.

Bad as are the conditions in Dublin, and hardly as they bear upon its working class, it is certain that Belfast pays so heavy a price for its 'prosperity' as to make one wonder if, after all, that prosperity is not too dearly bought. None acquainted with the lower-paid working class population of the two cities can have failed to note the extraordinary prevalence of illiteracy in Belfast as compared with Dublin. This illiteracy exists despite compulsory school attendance, and can only be accounted for by, first, the rapid growth of the former city, and second, the fact that the textile industries of Belfast depend upon women and child labour, making any real family life impossible, and any real control of young children ineffective amongst the mill population. Both these points are brought out in the last quotation we shall make from the *Report of the Belfast School Inspector* for 1911-12. He says, page 104:–

There is no doubt that a great many Belfast children do not attend school. The local schools may be overcrowded; the parents may remove so frequently that their children escape notice; factory life brings about a state of affairs which reduces parental influence to a minimum; some parents seem to have ceased to consider themselves responsible for the upbringing of their children. When the children are old enough, they get on half-time in the mills, and are then obliged to go to school. At a recent visit to a school attended by half-timers and other pupils, it was noticed that there were 104 half-timers in Standards I and II. These children were all over 12 years of age. Where were they between the age of 6 and 12?

To this evidence of the Inspector may be added the fact that half-timers really learnt nothing during the days they attend school, as, mixing with adults at work teaches them such habits of bravado and recklessness of speech and conduct as make them the despair of any and every teacher, and make their presence fatal to the discipline and educational value of the entire establishment.

To this picture of the result of the congestion of Belfast and the squalor of Dublin may be added a third, that of the depletion, the emptying of the rural districts of Ireland, and the awful loneliness that is gradually descending upon the once happy homes of the Gael as the capitalist system sucks the life's blood of the race. In Sligo we are told by the Report:–

There are some places where there are no children. Those who in the past did not emigrate, but remained at home, have grown up; and, confronted by the difficulty of subsistence, have never married.

In other places the young men and women emigrate year after year, and there are none left to help on the farm except the children, who are, therefore, kept away from school.

The problem presented by the schools is a problem that can only be settled in one way – viz., by the extension to those institutions of the democratic principle, and all that principle implies. We have had, ever since the establishment of the National Schools, an attempt to perform, by a mixture of bureaucracy and clericalism, what can only be accomplished by a full and complete application of democratic trust in the people. In order to cater to the rival churches the question of school accommodation has been left to the zeal of the various denominations, with the result that there are at least ten small schools where one large one could more efficiently and economically meet the requirements of the district. Instead of the magnificent public schools of American, Scottish or English towns we have in our cities squalid, unhealthy, wretched abominations, where teaching is a torture to the teacher, and learning a punishment to the taught. Where the democracy, functioning through a representative public body, would supply a competent staff of well-paid teachers, and splendidly-equipped, heated and lighted buildings, the present system of despotically-controlled education gives us a staff of wretchedly-paid teachers with no rights, but with duties continually increasing. These unfortunates are condemned to carry out the most important functions of modern society, in buildings totally unsuited for the purpose, badly ventilated and drained, and in most instances totally unheated save at the expense of the unfortunate head of the teaching staff.

The democracy of Ireland, amongst the first of the steps necessary to the regeneration of Ireland, must address itself to the extension of its ownership and administration to the Schools of Erin.

Whatever safeguards are necessary to ensure that the religious faith of the parents shall be respected in the children, will surely be adequately looked after by the representatives of a people to whom religion is a vital thing. Such safeguards are quite compatible with the establishment of popular control of schools, with the building and equipment of schools that shall be a joy to the scholar and an inspiration to the teacher, and with such a radical overhauling of the curriculum as shall ensure full recognition for the deeds and ideas of the men and women whose achievements mark the stages of the upward climb of the race, as their failures to achieve mark the equally important epochs of its martyrdom. When such Palaces of Education shall replace the torture houses at present doing duty as schools, when such honoured and loyally-paid teachers shall replace the sweated sufferers of to-day, and when such records as the progress of human enlightenment and freedom replace the record of royal, aristocratic and capitalistic feastings, slaughterings and dishonourings of the poor as pass muster for history at present, Erin may once more have reason to be proud of her scholars.

Chapter VIII

Labour and Co-operation in Ireland

In an earlier work, *Labour in Irish History*, we dealt at some length with an experiment in co-operation at Ralahine, County Clare, in the first half of the Nineteenth Century, and quoted extensively from contemporary witnesses to show the very great success achieved by the participants in, and promoters of that historic venture.

In the course of that description we were compelled to note the manner in which an attempt significant of so much, and revealing in the Irish nature so many untried possibilities of expansion and adaptability, had been ignored by successive generations of Irish historians and politicians.

These latter seem, indeed, always to have floated along the surface of events and to have recoiled from any investigation involving a challenging of the orthodox basis of society, with more timidity than that with which his Satanic Majesty is popularly supposed to recoil from holy water. Their one governing idea has, at all times, been to represent the Irish cause as but a variant of a reform movement in English society; that Ireland was restive because she was not treated with the same equal justice as England, and that if she was only so treated it would be found that Ireland was essentially orthodox, and lacking in sympathy for any attacks upon accepted social institutions.

Hence such historians and politicians have ever felt that the story of a co-operative experiment like that of Ralahine – an experiment initiated by believers in Utopian Socialism – required care in the telling lest its example became infectious, and was, in fact, better left untold.

Following along the same lines of action, when the modern co-operative movement was preached to the Irish farmers by the lecturers of the Irish Agricultural Organisation Society, when the literature prepared by Mr. George Russell, Father Finlay, S.J., Sir Horace Plunkett, and their fellow-labourers, was being pushed throughout Ireland, it was early discovered that their attempts to regenerate Irish agricultural life had no more bitter enemies than the political representatives of the Irish people, irrespective of their political colour.

The Unionist politicians opposed the co-operators because the movement tended to bring together Protestant and Catholic on a basis of friendly and fraternal helpfulness – a state of things that, if persisted in, would inevitably destroy that bigoted distrust and hatred upon which Unionism depended for its existence.

The Home Rulers opposed the co-operators upon the alleged grounds that their success in increasing the finances of the farmers would only redound to the advantage of the landlord, but really because the practice of co-operation would necessarily interfere with the profits of those leeches who, as gombeen men, middlemen and dealers of one kind or another in the small country towns, sucked the life-blood of the agricultural population around them.

Anyone acquainted with rural Ireland knows that, next to the merciless grinding by the landlord, the tenantry suffers most from the ruthless exploitation of the classes just mentioned, and that, indeed, the buying-out of the landlords in many cases served only to gorge still further the ever rapacious maw of those parasites upon rural life.

But whereas the landlords were ever regarded in Ireland as alien to Irish life, the gombeen men and their kind, from their position in the country towns, their ostentatious parade of religion and their loud-mouthed assertions of patriotism, were usually the dominant influences in the councils of the local Home Rule or other constitutional national organisation.

From all national organisations not constitutional, or 'respectable', they usually kept aloof, but this fact did not interfere with their power to dictate the attitude of the Irish Parliamentary representatives to every manifestation of Irish life. They were ever the local wirepullers, and, as such, posed as the representatives of the political thought of Ireland.

Thus it was in no wise strange that the Irish politicians as a whole were averse to all propaganda upon co-operative lines, and that as a writer in *The Irish Homestead*, says:–

Sir Horace Plunkett, Father Finlay and Mr. Anderson were assured that their ideas were quite unsuitable for Ireland, that the people wanted something else, that they were going contrary to Irish instincts, that their ideas might suit people like the Danes and Germans, but they must remember that Ireland had a unique character.

But neither was it strange that the co-operative principle had in itself an appealing force, quite sufficient to surmount this factitious opposition, although fifty meetings were held before a single society was formed.

Apart from the direct appeal founded upon self-interest, an appeal rooting itself in the necessities born of an ever-increasing difficulty in finding a profitable market for their commodities, the Irish farming population had long been accustomed to practical co-operation for given objects.

The sight of a whole countryside agreeing to build a cabin for some one left shelterless, to save the crops of a neighbour too sick to bring in his own, to dig the field of a widow, to raise money enough to enable a promising boy to get the education necessary to become a priest or a doctor, or in the olden days to bring in and support a hedge-schoolmaster, was not unfamiliar to Irish eyes, nor were the practical value of such kindly lessons lost to Irish understanding. And, in the days immediately preceding the co-operative propaganda, the Irish Land League had found the peasantry willing co-operators in a score of ways when such co-operation formed part of the campaign against landlordism.

Nor yet had all the insidious tendency of leaders, infatuated with capitalist doctrines, and too ignorant of their country's real history to understand its ancient institutions, ever been able to take from the peasantry the possession of traditions which kept alive in their midst the memory of the common ownership and common control of land by their ancestors – an ownership and control which were the very flower of co-operation.

Scattered around amongst them also they found the Catholic Church in all its convents and monasteries, practising co-operation alike upon the consumers' and producers' model, and with the element of personal profit or aggrandisement entirely eliminated.

When those considerations left the Irish agriculturalist still unconverted, there were still pressing upon him the forces born of economic development, urging him with an irresistible pressure toward a remodelling of his methods, and a reconsideration of his ideas. He found that he had no longer even a partial monopoly of the home market, but that, on the contrary, each development of the transport facilities of the world brought him a new danger, added a new menace to his anxiety. The inventor who enabled the steamship companies to shorten the time taken to convey agricultural products across the ocean; the engineer who laid down railroads which tapped new or backward lands and brought their crops to the ports of the world; the government which placed the resources of its scientists and its chemists at the disposal of its producers and merchants, all, all were new factors *bringing* new perils for him to face. In less than a generation New York, New Orleans, or the River Plate, the Black Sea and the Baltic have moved up, so to speak, to within easy commercial striking distance of the farmers of Ireland, and their merchandise confronts him in all his markets. From the Scandinavian countries the farmers, organised and taught with Government aid upon co-operative lines, were pouring in butter, cheese, and eggs, packed and forwarded in a manner infinitely superior to the old slipshod methods of the individual petty Irish farmer; from the South of France and the Channel Islands came all the varied output of highly-trained market gardeners working with all the advantages of climate and efficient transport service on their side, and all around the unfortunate Irish agriculturist was met with the competition of rivals much better trained, better educated, better led, better served, and by the demands of merchants and customers calling for greater nicety, greater cleanliness, greater despatch, and greater variety.

Under such pressure, face to face with such increasing competition, it is little to be wondered at that the propaganda of the co-operators eventually reached the Irish peasantry, despite all the obstacles raised and imaginary dangers invoked by the interested enemies of the new doctrine. To-day up and down through Ireland a network of co-operative societies has spread and is spreading amongst the peasantry, whilst new and more fruitful fields of enterprise are continually being opened up by their resourceful leaders and members. Over 100,000 Irish farmers are now organised in co-operative societies. We have co-operative creameries, co-operative marketing, co-operative banks, and projects for co-operative fishing are already well on their way.

In the towns co-operative societies of consumers have taken a firm foothold in the North and in the extreme South, whilst the result of the beneficent activities of the co-operative distributive societies during the great Dublin Labour Dispute left such an impression upon the minds of the workers in the Irish Labour movement, that a great crop of co-operative enterprises under the auspices of that movement may be confidently anticipated in the very near future.

Up to the present the participants in the co-operative movement amongst the agricultural population have, as is usual in Ireland, troubled themselves little about fashioning in their minds any form of ideal to result from their labours, but have instead attended strictly to the immediate needs of the moment. Amongst the leaders in the town movements, on the contrary, it may be said that as a rule their activities would be much less were it not for the ideal that inspires them. That ideal is the one common now to the militant workers of the world – a Co-operative Commonwealth.

The immediate difficulty if the two movements – i.e., of town and country, are not to remain strangers, with all the possibilities of developing from estrangement into hostility – will be to find a common basis of action in order that one may support and reinforce the other. Mr. George Russell, the gifted editor of *The Irish Homestead*, points out that the fact that the overwhelming proportion of Irish farmers employ no labour, but generally work their own farms, makes that problem not so difficult in Ireland as it would be in countries where the farmers were employers and therefore supposedly hostile to the claims of Labour. This idea, with all its implications, is worthy of careful examination.

Stated briefly it may be thus summed up: Since the great development of transatlantic and cross-sea competition, and the supplanting or curbing of the landlord, the chief problem for the Irish farmer is to find a good market where the balance will not be weighted against him. He can only find this by creating a market amongst a sympathetic and prosperous Irish working class. His products are not fancy products, they only appeal to the needs of the human stomach, and not to the whims, passions or fantasies of the imagination. A millionaire, having only one stomach, can only consume what one stomach requires, he cannot consume more of the staple products of our Irish farms than a well-paid tradesman would require and demand.

The dainties, delicacies, wines, &c., which go to make the dinner of the millionaire more costly than that of the tradesman are imported, and hence the greater cost of his dinner does not represent a greater demand for Irish agricultural products.

Thus the Irish farmer cannot increase the demand for his products by any support of the well-to-do, the millionaire, or the budding millionaire. On the contrary, every upward move of Labour in Ireland which adds to the income of the working class, and transforms its members from semi-starved slaves into well-paid toilers able to purchase a sufficiency of food, creates thousands or tens of thousands of new customers. Every defeat of Labour, accompanied by a reduction of purchasing power, lessens the demand for the products of Irish farmers; every victory of Labour increases the purchasing power of the working class and thus sends fresh customers into the Irish market. And if that victory for the Irish working class was won by the support of the co-operative farmers of Ireland, then every constituent of the Irish Labour movement would be morally bound to give preference to the commodities produced by their agricultural allies.

To that moral obligation the establishment and popularisation of co-operative stores under the aegis of the Labour movement would add another, that of self-interest.

Stocking the products of the agricultural co-operative societies in time of industrial peace, the workers would enjoy their credit in time of war; then the trades union in time of peace could invest its funds in the co-operative societies; in time of lock-outs or strikes it would fight with food guaranteed to its members by such societies which, for the food required, would be able to pledge their credit to the organised co-operative farming community.

Trade union funds, instead of being deposited in banks to be let out by those institutions to capitalist exploiters, could be placed to the credit of soundly conducted co-operative enterprises, developing the farmers and

63

aiding the resources of the toilers in town and country. In so doing the urban workers would know that, in helping to make life in the rural districts less unbearable, they were also helping to stem the flow of labour into the towns, thus increasing the security of their own position.

The idea is capable of almost infinite expansion, and not least amongst its attractions is the hope that the minds of Irish men and women, once set thus definitely in the direction of common work, common ownership, and democratically conducted industry, their thought would not cease from travelling that path until they had once more grasped the concept of an Ireland of whose powers, potentialities and gifts each should be an equal heir, in whose joys and cultures all should be sharers.

The letter to the Dublin Employers (printed in the Appendix), though it excited the wrath of all the tyrants and reactionaries in Ireland, served to win for Mr. Russell that hearing for the Co-operative position we have just outlined, which may yet make it in a double sense a historic document.

If, to that combination of agriculturalists and urban labourers we have just hinted at as a possibility of co-operation upon the economic field, we add the further possible development of an understanding upon the political field between these two groups of co-operators, we begin to realise the great and fundamental change now slowly maturing in our midst.

Such a political development may not, indeed probably will not, come soon, but the necessity of seeking legislation to aid their activities, as well as the necessity of preventing legislation to obstruct their activities, will force forward that development in due time.

Then, when to the easily organised labourers of the towns is added the immense staying power of the peasantry, and when representatives appear in the Halls of Legislature voicing their combined demands, the Party of Labour which will thus manifest itself will speak with a prophetic voice, when it proclaims its ideal for a regenerated Ireland – an Ireland re-conquered for its common people.

For the only true prophets are they who carve out the future which they announce.

Chapter IX

Re-Conquest – A Summing Up

Recent events in Ireland have gone far to show that the old lines of political demarcation no longer serve to express any reality in the lives of the people. The growth of unrest in the industrial field, the bitterness of industrial conflict, the maimer in which employers of the most varying political and religious faiths combine against the workers in the attempt to starve them into submission, and the marked increase in the fraternal feelings with which all classes of Labour regard each other, all serve to indicate that there is preparing in our midst the material for a new struggle on a national scale – a struggle fierce enough, deep enough, and enduring enough to obliterate completely all the old landmarks carried over from past political struggles into the new conditions.

In the great Dublin lock-out of 1913-1914 the manner in which the Dublin employers, overwhelmingly Unionist, received the enthusiastic and unscrupulous support of the entire Home Rule Press was a foretaste of the possibilities of the new combinations with which Labour in Ireland will have to reckon. The semi-radical phrases with which the middle-class Home Rule Press and politicians so often duped the public (and sometimes themselves) were seen to have no radical feeling behind them. Sham battle-cries of a sham struggle, they were hurriedly put out of sight the moment the war-cries of a real conflict rose upon the air.

From this lesson, as from the others already mentioned in this book, Labour must learn that the time has come for a new marshalling of forces to face the future. As the old political parties must go, so must many of the old craft divisions in the ranks of Labour. We have learned the value of the sympathetic strike; we must no longer allow craft divisions to fetter our hands and keep us from helping our brother or sister when they are attacked by the capitalist enemy. We must pursue the idea to its logical conclusion and work for the obliteration of all division of the forces of Labour on the industrial field.

The principle of complete unity upon the Industrial *plane* must be unceasingly sought after; the Industrial union embracing all workers in each industry must replace the multiplicity of unions which now hamper and restrict our operations, multiply our expenses and divide our forces in face of the mutual enemy. With the Industrial Union as our principle of action, branches can be formed to give expression to the need for effective supervision of the affairs of the workshop, shipyard, dock or railway; each branch to consist of the men and women now associated in Labour upon the same technical basis as our craft unions of to-day.

Add to this the concept of one Big Union embracing all, and you have not only the outline of the most effective form of combination for industrial warfare to-day, but also for Social Administration of the Co-operative Commonwealth of the future.

A system of society in which the workshops, factories, docks, railways, shipyards, &c., shall be owned by the nation, but administered by the Industrial Unions of the respective industries, organised as above, seems best calculated to secure the highest form of industrial efficiency, combined with the greatest amount of individual freedom from state despotism. Such a system would, we believe, realise for Ireland the most radiant hopes of all her heroes and martyrs.

Concurrently with the gradual shaping of our industrial activities towards the end of industrial union, Labour must necessarily attack the political and municipal citadels of power.

Every effort should be made to extend the scope of public ownership. As democracy invades and captures public powers public ownership will, of necessity, be transformed and infused with a new spirit. As Democracy enters, Bureaucracy will take flight. But without the power of the Industrial Union behind it, Democracy can only enter the State as the victim enters the gullet of the Serpent.

Therefore political power must, for the working classes, come straight out of the Industrial battlefield as the expression of the organised economic force of Labour; else it cannot come at all. With Labour properly organised upon the Industrial and political field, each extension of the principle of public ownership brings us nearer to the re-conquest of Ireland by its people; it means the gradual resumption of the common ownership of all Ireland by all the Irish – the realisation of Freedom.

Not the least of the many encouraging signs given to the world during the great Dublin Labour dispute just mentioned was the keen and sympathetic interest shown by the 'intellectuals' in the fortunes of the workers. In itself this was a phenomenon in Ireland. Until then, there had been discovered no means of bridging the gap between the Irish workers who toiled as ordinary day labourers, and those other workers whose toil was upon the intellectual plane, and whose remuneration kept them generally free from the actual pressure of want.

In other European countries the Socialist movement had brought these two elements together, in organised defensive and aggressive warfare against the brutal regime of the purse; but in Ireland the fight for national freedom had absorbed the intellect of the one, and prevented the development of the necessary class-consciousness on the part of the other.

But when the belief that some form of national freedom was about to be realised spread in Ireland, and consequently the minds of all began to turn to consideration of the uses to which that freedom might be put, the possibility of co-operation between these two classes became apparent to the thoughtful patriot and reformer.

The incidents accompanying the great Labour struggle furnished just the necessary common denominator to establish relations between the two.

We have no doubt that it will be found in Ireland, as it has already been found in Italy, that the co-operation of the wage labourers and their intellectual comrades will create an uplifting atmosphere of social helpfulness of the greatest benefit in the work of national regeneration. We have in Ireland, particularly outside of the industrial districts of the North, a greater proportion of professional, literary and artistic people than is to be found in any European country except Italy, and, without enquiring too closely into the cause of this undue proportion, it may be predicted that its existence will serve the cause of Labour in Ireland.

Arising out of the same struggle, what may yet develop into a perfect understanding and concert of action was opened up between the Urban labourers and the apostles of co-operation amongst the agricultural population of Ireland. The great genius and magnetic personality of Mr. Russell, editor of *The Irish Homestead*, brought to the long-neglected toilers of Dublin a new conception – viz., that the co-operative societies which had been so long and so successfully propagating themselves throughout the agricultural areas of the country, might yet be linked up with the fortunes of the industrial workers in such a manner that, each serving the other's temporary needs, they could between them lay the groundwork of a new social order.

Almost throughout all historic periods there has been a latent antagonism between town and country; the Socialist has predicted that the Socialist state of the future will put an end to that antagonism by bringing the advantages of the city to the toiler in the country; Mr. Russell foresees, however, a co-operation in which the city and the country shall merge in perfecting methods of fraternal production and distribution that shall serve, first to enable each to combat capitalism, and finally to supplant it. Such a development of co-operative effort between the workers of town and country would be a great achievement, and we can at least bespeak for the effort *and* the constant support of every friend of progress in Ireland.

In conclusion, we may say that this hope of co-operation between town and country for the purpose of common regeneration is typical of the hopes and possibilities now opening up to the workers of Ireland.

Everywhere we see friends, where formerly we met only suspicion and distrust; and we realise that the difference in the attitude with which Labour is regarded now to what it met formerly, is the difference with which the world at large treats those who simply claim its pity, and those who are strong and self-reliant enough to enforce its respect.

Labour in Ireland tends to become more and more self-reliant, and in its self-reliance it discovers its strength. Out of such strong self-reliance it develops a magnetism, which will draw to it more and more support from all the adherents of all the causes which in their entirety make for a regenerated Ireland.

The Gaelic Leaguer realises that capitalism did more in one century to destroy the tongue of the Gael than the sword of the Saxon did in six; the apostle of self-reliance amongst Irishmen and women finds no more earnest exponents of self-reliance than those who expound it as the creed of Labour; the earnest advocates of co-operation find the workers stating their ideals as a co-operative commonwealth; the earnest teacher of Christian morality sees that in the co-operative commonwealth alone will true morality be possible, and the fervent patriot learns that his hopes of an Ireland re-born to National life is better stated, and can be better and more completely realised, in the Labour movement for the Re-Conquest of Ireland.

Our readers will help forward the purpose of this book, and hasten the coming of the good results that should flow from the happy synchronising of facts just alluded to, if they will always remember that the objective aimed at is to establish, in the minds of men and women of Ireland, the necessity of giving effective expression, politically and socially, to the right of the community (all) to control, for the good of all, the industrial activities of each, and to endow such activities with the necessary means.

This, historically speaking, will mean the enthronement of the Irish nation as the supreme ruler and owner of itself, and all things necessary to its people – supreme alike against the foreigner and the native usurping ownership, and the power dangerous to freedom that goes with ownership.

JAMES CONNOLLY.

Appendix 1

The Protestant View

As a further commentary upon the claim that the Williamite forces at the Battle of the Boyne fought for Civil and Religious liberty, the following analyses of the spirit of the Protestant sects have a grim humour of their own:–

Episcopalianism

The Church of England continued to be for more than 150 years the servile handmaid of monarchy, the steady enemy of public liberty.

The divine right of kings and the duty of passively obeying all their commands, were her favourite tenets. She held these tenets firmly through times of oppression, persecution and licentiousness, while law was trampled down, while judgment was perverted, while the people were eaten as if they were bread. – Macaulay, *Essays*.

Anglicanism (Episcopalianism) was, from the beginning, at once the most servile and the most efficient agent of tyranny. Endeavouring, by the assistance of temporal authority and by the display of worldly power, to realise in England the same position as Catholicism had occupied in Europe, she naturally flung herself on every occasion into the arms of the civil power.

No other Church so uniformly betrayed and trampled upon the liberties of her country. In all those fiery trials through which English liberty has passed since the Reformation, she invariably cast her influence into the scale of tyranny, supported and eulogised every attempt to violate the Constitution, and wrote the fearful sentence of eternal condemnation upon the tombs of the martyrs of freedom. – W.E.H. Lecky, *Rationalism in Europe*.

Presbytherianism

"While England was breaking loose from her ancient superstitions, and advancing with gigantic strides along the road of knowledge, Scotland still cowered, with a willing submission, before her clergy. Never was a mental servitude more complete; and never was a tyranny maintained with more inexorable barbarity.

"Supported by public opinion, the Scottish ministers succeeded in overawing all opposition; in prohibiting the faintest expressions of adverse opinions; in prying into and controlling the most private concerns of domestic life; in compelling everyone to conform absolutely to all the ecclesiastical regulations they enjoined; and in, at last, directing the whole scope and current of legislation.

"They maintained their ascendancy over the popular mind by a system of religious terrorism, which we can now barely conceive." – W.E.H. Lecky, *Rationalism in Europe*.

Appendix II.

Report of Dublin Housing Commission (1914)

We fully endorse the evidence given by many witnesses that the surroundings of a tenement house, in which there can be no privacy, and in which the children scarcely realise the meaning of the word 'home', form the worst possible atmosphere for the upbringing of the younger generation, who, as one of the witnesses stated, acquire a precocious knowledge of evil from early childhood.

Death-Rate in Dublin

While there has been a slight reduction in the death-rate in Dublin from all causes in recent years, still the death-rate for the year 1911, the last year for which complete returns are available for the United Kingdom, was higher than in any of the larger centres of population in England, Wales or Scotland, and we fear that, until the housing problem is adequately dealt with, no substantial reduction in the death-rate may be hoped for.

Speaking generally, the tenement house property in Dublin is owned by a large number of small owners, who, as Mr. Travers told us at an interview subsequent to the inquiry, hold at the most about forty persons each per house.

The principal owners of tenement houses sitting as members of the Corporation are Alderman G. O'Reilly, Alderman Corrigan, and Councillor Crozier, who are returned to us in the evidence as either owning, or being interested in, nine, nineteen, and eighteen tenement houses respectively, and in four, thirteen, and one small houses; while ten other members of the Corporation own or are interested in one to three tenement houses, and Alderman O'Connor owns or is interested in two tenement houses and six small houses.

We regret to have to report that some of the property owned by the three first-named gentlemen, and from which they are deriving rents, is classed as third-class property by the sanitary staff, or, in other words, that it is unfit for human habitation.

A feature which makes this all the more discreditable is that actually, on some of this class of property, both Alderman O'Reilly and Alderman Corrigan are receiving rebates of taxes under Section 75 of the Corporation Act of 1890. Councillor Crozier is also receiving a rebate on property which, though not classed as being unfit for human habitation, is not, however, in our opinion, in such a condition of repair as to warrant a rebate being given, and does not comply with the express conditions required by the Corporation.

In two instances, affecting twelve dwellings belonging to Alderman Corrigan, the property was certified by the sanitary sub-officer as not fit for a rebate, but was subsequently passed as fit on the authority of Sir Charles Cameron. In the first instance, comprising ten dwellings, it was stated that the drains were not properly trapped or ventilated, and that the entire premises were not kept clean or in a good state of repair.

In the other case, comprising two dwellings, it was stated there was not proper and sufficient yard space, and that the tenants had no water-closet accommodation, and were compelled to use the water-closet accommodation attached to another set of cottages.

Mr. Corrigan admits having done nothing to the drains in the former case, after the inspection by the sanitary sub-officer, and the evidence of Mr. Travers would show that the sanitary accommodation provided for the use of the tenants in the latter case, which was, as stated, used in common by the occupants of other cottages, consisted of only three water-closets for eighty-one persons.

Sir Charles Cameron stated in his evidence that he accepted full responsibility in these cases.

Closet Accommodation

The plea of the Corporation, in regard to the insufficiency of their powers, would have considerably more force were it supported by evidence of a rigid administration of existing powers. The facts, however, would go to show that Sir Charles Cameron has taken on himself a dispensing power in regard 259 to the closet accommodation stated to be necessary under the by-laws relating to tenement houses, and we have ascertained that out of 5,322 tenement houses there are 627 with sanitary accommodation at the rate of one closet for 20 to 24 persons, 299 with accommodation at the rate of one closet for 25 to 29 persons, 145 with accommodation at the rate of one closet for 30 to 31 persons, 58 with accommodation at the rate of one closet for 35 to 39 persons, and 32 with accommodation at the rate of one closet for 40 or more persons.

Small Houses

So far we have dealt with the condition of life in tenement houses, but we have still to deal with those obtaining in what are termed by the sanitary staff of the Corporation second and third-class houses, other than tenement houses. Some of these structures scarcely deserve the name of house, and could be more aptly described as shelters. A number of them are erected in narrow areas almost surrounded by high buildings, with alleys or passages, which in some cases are scarcely more than nine or ten feet wide, as a means of approach. These houses have, as a rule, no separate closet accommodation, but one or two, or occasionally more, closets situated somewhere in the vicinity are common to the occupants of the cottages or anyone who likes to use them, while the water tap, situated close by, is also common.

The houses are, therefore, as far as sanitary arrangements are concerned, in much the same category as the tenement houses, and in all cases where we inspected, in which the closets were common, they were exceedingly dirty and badly kept, and unfit for use by persons of cleanly habits.

These rows of cottages may be said to suffer from many of the drawbacks of tenement houses, and they have the added disadvantage referred to, of being in some cases surrounded by high walls and buildings, which shut out light and air.

Appendix III

To the Masters of Dublin – An Open Letter

by George W. Russell (A.E.)

The Irish Times, Tuesday, October 7th, 1913

SIRS, –

I address this warning to you, the aristocracy of industry in this city, because, like all aristocracies, you tend to grow blind in long authority, and to be unaware that you and your class and its every action are being considered and judged day by day, by those who have power to shake or overturn the whole Social Order; and whose restlessness in poverty to-day is making our industrial civilisation stir like a quaking bog. You do not seem to realise, that your assumption that you are answerable to yourselves alone for your actions in the industries you control, is one that becomes less and less tolerable in a world so crowded with necessitous life. Some of you have helped Irish farmers to upset a landed aristocracy in this island, an aristocracy richer and more powerful in its sphere than you are in yours, with its roots deep in history. They, too, as a class, though not all of them, were scornful or neglectful of the workers in the industry by which they profited; and to many who knew them in their pride of place, and thought them all-powerful, they are already becoming a memory, the good disappearing together with the bad. If they had done their duty by those from whose labour came their wealth, they might have continued unquestioned in power and prestige for centuries to come. The relation of landlord and tenant is not an ideal one, but any relations in a social order will endure, if there is infused into them some of that spirit of human sympathy which qualifies life for immortality. Despotisms endure while they are benevolent, and aristocracies while *noblesse oblige* is not a phrase to be referred to with a cynical smile. Even an oligarchy might be permanent if the spirit of human kindness, which harmonises all things otherwise incompatible, is present.

You do not seem to read history so as to learn its lessons. That you are an uncultivated class was obvious from recent utterances of some of you upon art. That you are incompetent men in the sphere in which you arrogate imperial powers is certain, because for many years, long before the present uprising of labour, your enterprises have been dwindling in the regard of investors; and this while you have carried them on in the cheapest labour market in these islands, with a labour reserve always hungry and ready to accept any pittance. You are bad citizens, for we rarely, if ever, hear of the wealthy among you endowing your city with the munificent gifts which it is the pride of merchant princes in other cities to offer, and Irishmen not of your city who offer to supply the wants left by your lack of generosity are met with derision and abuse. Those who have economic power have civic power also, yet you have not used the power that was yours to right what was wrong in the evil administration of this city. You have allowed the poor to be herded together, so that one thinks of certain places in Dublin as of a pestilence. There are twenty thousand rooms, in each of which live entire families, and sometimes more, where no functions of the body can be concealed and delicacy and modesty are creatures that are stifled ere they are born. The obvious duty of you in regard to these things you might have left undone, and it would be imputed to ignorance or forgetfulness; but your collective and conscious action as a class in the present labour dispute, has revealed you to the world in so malign an aspect that the mirror must be held up to you, so that you may see yourselves as every humane person sees you.

The conception of yourselves as altogether virtuous and wronged is, I assure you, not at all the one which onlookers hold of you. No doubt, you have rights on your side. No doubt, some of you suffered without just cause. But nothing which has been done to you cries aloud to Heaven for condemnation as your own actions. Let me show you how it seems to those who have followed critically the dispute, trying to weigh in a balance the rights and wrongs. You were within the rights society allows you, when you locked out your men and insisted on the fixing of some principle to adjust your future relations with labour, when the policy of labour made it impossible for some of you to carry on your enterprises. Labour desired the fixing of some such principle as much as you did. But, having once decided on such a step, knowing how many thousands of men, women, and children, nearly one-third of the population of this city, would be affected, you should not have let one day to have passed without unremitting endeavours to find a solution of the problem.

What did you do? The representatives of labour unions in Great Britain met you, and you made of them a preposterous, an impossible demand,

and, because they would not accede to it, you closed the Conference: you refused to meet them further; you assumed that no other guarantees than those you asked were possible, and you determined deliberately in cold anger, to starve out one-third of the population of this city, to break the manhood of the men by the sight of the suffering of their wives and the hunger of their children. We read in the Dark Ages of the rack and the thumb-screw. But these iniquities were hidden and concealed from the knowledge of men, in dungeons and torture chambers. Even in the Dark Ages humanity could not endure the sight of such suffering, and it learnt of such misuses of power by slow degrees, through rumour, and, when it was certain, it razed its Bastilles to their foundations. It remained for the twentieth century and the capital city of Ireland to see an oligarchy of four hundred masters deciding openly upon starving one hundred thousand people, and refusing to consider any solution except that fixed by their pride. You, masters, asked men to do that which masters of labour in any other city in these islands had not dared to do. You insolently demanded of those men who were members of a trade union that they should resign from that union; and from those who were not members you insisted on a vow that they would never join it.

Your insolence and ignorance of the rights conceded to workers universally in the modern world were incredible, and as great as your inhumanity. If you had between you collectively a portion of human soul as large as a threepenny-bit, you would have sat night and day with the representatives of labour, trying this or that solution of the trouble, mindful of the women and children, who at least were innocent of wrong against you. But no! You reminded Labour you could always have your three meals a day while it went hungry. You went into conference again with representatives of the State, because, dull as you are, you knew public opinion would not stand your holding out. You chose as your spokesman the bitterest tongue that ever wagged in this island, and then, when an award was made by men who have an experience in industrial matters a thousand times transcending yours, who have settled disputes in industries so great that the sum of your petty enterprises would not equal them, you withdraw again; and will not agree to accept their solution, and fall back again upon your devilish policy of starvation. Cry aloud to Heaven for new souls! The souls you have got, cast upon the screen of publicity, appear like the horrid and writhing creatures enlarged from the insect world, and revealed to us by the microscope.

You may succeed in your policy and ensure your own damnation by your victory. The men whose manhood you have broken will loathe you, and will always be brooding and scheming to strike a fresh blow. The children will be taught to curse you. The infant being moulded in the womb will have breathed into its starved body the vitality of hate. It is not they – it is you who are blind Samsons pulling down the pillars of the social order. You are sounding the death-knell of autocracy in industry. There was autocracy in political life, and it was superseded by democracy. So surely will democratic power wrest from you the control of industry. The fate of you, the aristocracy of industry, will be as the fate of the aristocracy of land, if you do not show that you have some humanity still among you. Humanity abhors, above all things, a vacuum in itself, and your class will be cut off from humanity as the surgeon cuts the cancer and the alien growth from the body. Be warned ere it is too late.

Yours, &c.,
A.E.

DUBLIN, October 6th, 1913.

Other books from

Freemasonry

Look to the East
- Ralph P. Lester
Morals and Dogma
- Albert Pike
Duncan's Ritual and Monitor of Freemasonry
- Malcolm C. Duncan
Ritual of the Order of the Eastern Star
- F. A. Bell
Meaning of Masonry
- W.L Wilmshurst
Exposition of Freemasonry – Illustrated
- WM. Morgan

Philosophy

Politics
- Aristotle
Republic
- Plato
The Advancement of Learning
- Francis Bacon
The Interpretation of Dreams
- Sigmund Freud
HAGAKURE - Selections (The Way of the Samurai)
- Yamamoto Tsunetomo

Autobiographys

Autobiography of Ben Franklin
Autobiography of Charles Darwin
Autobiography of John Stuart Mill

Religious

Book of Jasher
- J.H. Parry
The Way to Christ
- Jacob Boehme
Imitation of Christ
- Thomas A Kempis
The First Book of Adam and Eve
- Rutherford H. Platt

Miscellaneous

The Devil's Dictionary
- Ambrose Bierce
Ancient Egypt - The Light of the World
- Gerald Massey
Natural Magick
- John Baptista Porta
The Two Babylons
- Alexander Hislop

And many, many more titles available at

www.nuvisionpublications.com

Printed in the United States
124503LV00009BA/8/A

9 781595 478993